Sharper
Edges

Sharper Edges

STORIES BEYOND
HIGH AND WILD PLACES

ANDY de KLERK

SUNBIRD

First Edition 2007
Sunbird Publishers (Pty) Ltd
P O Box 6836
Roggebaai 8012
Cape Town, South Africa

Registration number: 4850177827

www.sunbirdpublishers.co.za

Copyright © published edition 2007: Sunbird Publishers
Copyright © text 2007 Andy de Klerk
Copyright © photography as credited on page 196
Copyright © illustrations Peter Samuelson

PUBLISHER: Natanya Mulholland
EDITOR: Lisa Templeton
PROOFREADER: Sean Fraser
DESIGNER: Pete Bosman
ILLUSTRATOR: Peter Samuelson

Reproduction by Resolution Colour (Pty) Ltd, Cape Town, South Africa
Printed and bound by Tien Wah Press (Pte) Ltd, Singapore

ISBN-10 1-919938-48-6
ISBN-13 978-1-919938-48-6

1 2 3 4 5 6 7 8 9 10

To Julie and Ed

Contents

Foreword

By Ed February

Strange how one can clearly remember some things that happened more than 20 years ago, yet can't find the car keys you had in your hand not five minutes before. That's me, always forgetting things, but I can still very clearly remember the details of that first route Andrew and I climbed together on Table Mountain. Greg Lacey and I had bounced leads through the difficult bottom sections with the kid radiating energy and excitement only restrained by my growling at him. When we finally unleashed him on the last pitch, a superb grade 19 overhanging crack, I started a cry that was to become a refrain over the next 20-years. "PUT SOME GEAR IN." Not thinking that those following might not find it as easy, Andrew never placed protective gear in the rock if he found the climbing to be easy. Over the next few years I was often faced with an enormous swing through space following Andrew on what he felt was an easy pitch. These situations frequently left me completely terrified as I contemplated a vividly imagined arc terminating in the unyielding surface of an adjoining wall. Within a short space of time after meeting Andrew my beautiful jet-black afro hairstyle started showing the first streaks of grey brought on by these intense bouts of sheer terror.

We opened two new routes at Spring Buttress on Table Mountain that day, after which I knew that the kid was going to be good, very good. I hadn't seen anybody that good since climbing with Dave Cheesmond almost 10 years before. The only problem was that he was too enthusiastic and although talented still had a lot to learn. Greg and I chatted over a beer that night and agreed, me more reluctantly than he, that the kid had to climb with us before he did something stupid and killed himself. I had no idea at the time of the strong bond of friendship that would form between us. Eight years later Andrew left South Africa to live in the USA and a little bit of me left with him. By then he was the finest alpinist to leave these shores, after he had established some of the hardest rock climbs in the country. Routes such as Dream Street Rose on Elsies Peak in Fish Hoek, which he opened in 1985, are still considered modern-day test pieces.

I was truly depressed when Andrew left South Africa and in fact didn't climb for a while. We didn't lose contact though and I knew that my attitude was one of selfishness. There was no doubt in my mind that working in America was the best way to finance his climbing. Julie was also the best partner he could find. Not someone who had to tolerate his climbing but someone with whom he could share that climbing. For almost 10 years Andrew lived outside South Africa having many adventures on almost every continent on earth, firmly establishing himself as an international figure in mountaineering. Andrew and I still continued to have outings together but it is Julie who accompanied him on some of his finest.

Here Andrew, a legend in South African mountaineering circles, takes us on some of his journeys. Rather than focus on the technical aspects of the climbing and BASE jumping, for which he is famous, this rather unusual book is more focused on the why. Andrew has always been a deep thinker and philosopher, and so from Gasherbrum IV in the Himalayas to the birth of his children, through his writing, Andrew tries to understand what he is and where he is going. In doing this, he shares a bit of his inner self with us, a part of the soul very few of us lay bare. We have never discussed this but he knows that I have always hated his BASE jumping. In this book I get the beginnings of an understanding of why he went there and that he is considering stopping. It is an interesting mix of life's adventures as told from the heart of a truly remarkable man.

The stories I have to tell take a journey over the sharper edges of the world, and they cover a lot of ground: from climbing mountains, through BASE jumping off them, to change and family life. In some my heart and soul have been laid bare, while others describe the unique friendships of the rope and the profound adventure of travelling to new places and seeking challenges in the high and wild parts of the world.

The common thread is my search for simple truths about what we do and why we do it. Climbers and BASE jumpers are intimately embroiled in the exciting life, so that that life becomes absolutely normal, though few people can understand it and most see it as downright crazy.

In a very personal way, these stories try to deconstruct that extreme world in order to understand what lies beneath our ambitions, our motivations and the whole experience. I am trying to see it objectively from the perspective of someone who has, finally, grown up, changed, and cornered a view from both outside and inside.

I have always been entranced by beauty, whether it's a quality in a person, the landscape or how we construct the world, and the essence of these stories is that life itself is beautiful. But that's the way I am, always having to go the most difficult way around to find the answers to the simplest questions.

There are a few people I would like to thank for making this book possible: editor Lisa Templeton, whose sensitivity made my stories and the people in them come to life, publisher Natanya Mulholland for her shrewd and unwavering focus on the big picture, designer Pete Bosman for making sense of the mess, and artist Pete Samuelson for the beautiful illustrations and the moments of peace we shared in the storm of BASE jumping.

And Julie Brugger and Ed February for the simple joy we shared in the hills.

AdK

There are three rules of alpinism:

1. Expect to Fail
2. Never Give Up
3. Take One Bite at a Time

Bird People

The call came on my cell phone at dusk as I navigated the first spoonful of mashed banana into my baby daughter's toothless mouth. It was my friend and fellow BASE jumper Nick "Moose" Good, sounding urgent and uncharacteristically economic with his words. "Karl's had a cliff-strike on Table Mountain. I'll pick you up in five minutes." It was uncanny, but for the past few weeks I'd had a nagging feeling that someone was going to get hurt BASE jumping. Every time my phone rang, I'd felt a sense of dread at the shrill sound. This call had caught me by surprise, but the important things always do: they catch you off balance when you're not concentrating. I handed the spoon to my wife Charlotte and quickly gathered my gear.

The word cliff-strike instils terror in any BASE jumper. It makes our blood run cold, our hearts beat faster and our instincts scream: "No, it won't happen to me. It can't." But it does happen, too often for comfort. And when it does, there's nothing you can do except react as best you can. Jumping off fixed objects with a parachute is a risky business, but all BASE jumpers know that and accept it. Our parachutes have to open with power and startling rapidity, but there is a risk that one side will inflate faster than the other, opening the canopy, horrifyingly, to face directly into the cliff. Sometimes, with a very quick reaction, you can turn the parachute away in time, but sometimes not. And then it all goes to hell in a crunching cliff-strike.

Moose pulled up outside my house in his truck and we drove into the warm autumn night, talking about BASE jumping. It's an addictive, exhilarating experience jumping off stationary objects, things like buildings, antennae, bridges and cliffs with a parachute, so we all did it despite the inherent risk. But virtually everyone I knew who BASE jumped had been injured in some way. And now Karl. Karl Hayden had become a good friend over the six years I had known him and we had done hundreds of BASE jumps together. Our nickname for him was "The General", because he was the father of BASE jumping in South Africa, the first to jump off Table Mountain and a host of other towering objects around the country, and the most motivated person in our tightly knit clan. He inspired us all with his calm, martial precision when it came to BASE jumping. A 45-year-old deep-sea diver, Karl is no stranger to the sharper edge of life. After surfacing from a month beneath the frigid depths of the North Sea oil rigs, it is little wonder that he would want to spend his time in the sky. Karl is also a very experienced skydiver, meticulous in his preparation and parachute packing, conservative in his judgement about conditions and very cautious in his outlook.

There were flashing red lights and crackling radios as we pulled into the parking lot at the lower cable-car station. Dion Tromp, leader of the High Angle Rescue Team, and his crew were calmly and methodically organising their gear for Karl's rescue. I had called Karl on his cell phone while we were driving and he had been quite unlike his normal self. Speaking with his jaw clenched he gave me a summary of his injuries and said he was stable, but I could hear by the strain in his voice he was badly hurt. I was worried. But even so, we were all calm, orderly and thorough as the rescue team stepped into the cable-car and it slid silently into the darkness high above the city lights, stopping in mid-air at the foot of the precipitous cliffs some way below the upper cable station. This was our exit point. From here we rappelled straight out of the door of the stationary cable-car, each member of the team leaning backwards to drop noiselessly down to the dark ledge below.

I knew exactly where Karl would be. How many times had I looked down in freefall at that spot, where one of us would, inevitably, come to an abrupt and bone-jarring stop? The Table Mountain jump is low and scary. It starts on a ledge of white rock that juts out from the mountain's flat top. A six-step run and a leap is all it takes to send you sailing over the edge of the sheer 150-metre drop. It's like jumping from a 45-storey building. It takes three seconds of freefall to cover a quarter of that distance and then it's time to deploy your canopy. Allow another two seconds for the parachute to open, and then you're very close to the place of impact. The margins are very tight. But despite the fear factor, we had all done it often.

I always look down when I jump and I've never quite worked out why. Ground rush is mesmerising, almost hypnotic, as you plummet towards the earth and it seems to race up to meet you. The opportunity to open is razor thin: a second can mean the difference between life and death. They found Xavier Bongard, an experienced Swiss BASE jumper and big wall climber, at the bottom of Lauterbrunnen, a 300-metre cliff in Switzerland, with his parachute unopened and pilot chute still stowed. He had made no attempt to open it, and no one will ever know why. I don't know either, but I think I understand.

As Moose and I scuttled through the darkness along Africa ledge, past The Lily Pond, my headlight beam caught the eyes of a small grey pigeon quietly perched on a rock. We stared at each other for a second, its two unblinking, unmoving red eyes looking directly into mine. The bird had a broken wing, folded back on itself at a funny angle. I picked it up in both hands and moved it out of the path. The bird never flinched, never moved and never resisted. Resigned to its fate, those two red eyes watched me impassively. I had to leave that little bird because one of ours was also broken and we had to get to him. I still wonder what became of that bird. What happens to birds that can't fly anymore?

I have also been a BASE casualty, a bird that couldn't fly. I have also broken myself and I too have needed rescuing by Dion and his team. Most of my BASE-jumping friends have had a serious accident at some stage. But, like a moth to a flame, I just couldn't keep away. The flame of risk burned bright, it was mesmerising. My attraction to BASE spirals back to the summer of 1999, when BASE jumping first rocketed into South Africa. Back in those Halcyon days there were four of us: Karl, Shaun Smith, John van Schalkwyk and me leading the fray, opening new sites and finding new cliffs, buildings, antennae, anything high to jump off. Some of it was legal, like the many cliffs and bridges we jumped, but others not, like antennae in the nuclear power station and tall buildings in the city centre. We were a pretty eccentric group, with totally divergent dispositions and professions; Karl a diver, Shaun a film producer, John a Special Task Force policeman, and myself a cabinetmaker, but we were united by our burning desire to BASE jump. It was the summer of our naïveté. We all knew that BASE jumping was a high-risk activity, but we didn't consider that an accident could ever happen to us. We did so many jumps that summer. We lived, ate, slept and dreamt those precious seconds suspended in space, but so close to the ground. It was an addiction, and a curse, to be able to visit that untethered world, each time emerging unscathed to walk away on both legs and do it again. That summer brought the four of us together in a way unique to high and risky places. But you can only enjoy that innocent luck for so long.

Of the four of us, I was the first to crash out of the sky, and it happened on an old climbing nemesis of mine, Milner Peak, in the Hex River Mountains. Two hours by road from Cape Town a dusty farm track turns off the highway and winds through leafy vineyards and fruit orchards to end abruptly at a weir. The Hex River mountain range rises up thousands of metres from here in tortured geographic relief. Three hours of walking up a bushy kloof takes you to the base of Milner Peak; a twin tiered amphitheatre of steep red rock. It's only five hours from Cape Town, but could very well be on another planet. It's big, very wild and very remote.

There are two cliffs you can jump off. The lower amphitheatre is a 200-metre bowl scooped out of overhanging sandstone from which a waterfall plunges. Above this is a steep slope that climbs to the upper wall, a 400-metre gently tapering scoop below the summit trig beacon.

Milner Peak contains all the essential aspects for adventure: big cliffs in a remote back country setting, with some of the best climbing and BASE jumping in the world secretly tucked into the folds of its contorted sheerness. It is a beautiful place, delicate and fragile, and yet incredibly tough, just like the human body. Milner can be friendly and benign, just as it can be vicious, savage and remote. It all depends on what happens when you're there.

Some weeks before my accident Shane Willard, a Special Task Force policeman friend of John's, crash-landed in the rocks in the landing area at the base of the lower wall. It was his fourth BASE jump. Shane's nickname in the force is "Staaldraad" (Steel Wire) and he's tough: not someone you would want to meet in a dark alley unless he's on your side. His ankle swelled up immediately and then turned purple and we all knew it was broken, but he injected himself with the powerful painkiller Pethadine and insisted on walking out. We carried his gear and watched him fight the pain, but he made it. It took six months and two operations before he could walk properly again.

The day I crashed I knew I was going to get hurt, but I jumped anyway. I can usually visualise an entire jump from launch to landing, but this time I kept drawing a blank when I tried to see myself coming in to land. Over and over I tried to picture it, but I never finished the jump in my mind before I finally went over the edge. There were five beautiful seconds of freefall, as I gazed down at three rocks in the intense green patch directly below me. Then I opened my parachute and flew into the turbulent gusting winds that swirl around the base of Milner Peak. I misjudged the final approach and instead of landing on our small open landing area, I landed a metre short of it, crashing into a rocky ravine. It was over in a flash. I ploughed very hard and very fast into a rock with both feet outstretched to take the impact. I later found out all about tibia plateau fractures: the edge of my knee joint had sheared off, something common on high impact injuries.

I heard my knee break, a distinctive crack and an odd silence afterwards. I didn't feel any pain as Karl ran up to me and asked: "Are you OK?". "I'm OK", I replied, but I wasn't really. I looked down and saw my hands begin to shake, and I knew then that I had gone too far.

I kept telling myself that my knee was just sprained, even though I knew it wasn't. It swelled up like a football and I tied my scarf around it to compress the swelling. Then I went up and finished bolting and retrieving my ropes from a climbing route that I had been opening on the lower wall. I told Karl and Shaun that I would be fine in the morning even though I knew I wouldn't be. I swallowed every pain-killer we could find in the camp and went to bed early and still I didn't sleep a wink.

Early the next morning I tried my hardest to do what Staaldraad had done and walk out with the aid of a crutch but I didn't get very far. It took me two hours to cover 400 metres, a distance that would normally have taken ten minutes. I hauled myself onto a rock, lit a cigarette, and realised that I couldn't help myself any more; it would take me a week to crawl out and I would now have to rely on my friends. It was the first time I would need to be rescued, ever. The sun was warm and my knee throbbed. Giving up was a big relief. Finally it was out of my hands. Shaun ran out and made the call for help, while I dragged myself back to a big fig tree at the base of the wall and Karl and I sat there for the rest of the day and waited. I felt mellow and resigned to fate and, as long as I didn't have move my leg, I could have stayed there forever. Just before dusk we heard the throb of a helicopter. It circled for a long time searching for us – it was before GPS coordinates, which could have pinpointed our position – and it eventually landed on a high ridge quite a long way away from us. Brent Jennings and a paramedic from the High Angle Rescue Team walked into our camp several hours later with two-way radios, communications and a trauma kit and then it was all over. The Tramacet painkiller they injected into my arm that night made me sleep like a newborn baby.

The next day a big Alouette helicopter from the 22nd Air Force Squadron landed at the base of the lower wall to collect me in a whistling fury of turbine-fuelled power. The first person I saw was Dion Tromp crouching at the door. And he, together with his team, Douw Steyn, Brent Jennings and Dr Rik de Decker; lifted me into the helicopter. They were the same strong, capable, selfless men who would come to the aid of my friends in the years to follow. I was so glad to see them, so ashamed, so thankful that they had come to fetch me, and, for the first time in my life, helpless and broken.

In the quiet months of reflection afterwards, I kept rehearsing that strong bone snap. It healed, as our bodies always do, but it was never the same again. Over the next three years Dion and the High Angle Rescue Team flew in to Milner a few more times to rescue BASE-jumping friends of mine. First, Pete Samuelson, who is very experienced, needed rescuing after clipping a rock and breaking his foot while coming in to land. And then, far more traumatically, the young skydiver, Lisa Beasley, who suffered a devastating cliff-strike. It all happened in an instant. A blink of the eye, and a young life was changed forever. Lisa jumped off the lower wall and her parachute opened and swung straight into the cliff face. There was nothing she could do. She smashed into the cliff three times and hit a ledge on the way down before coming to a stop in the camp site directly below the exit point. Her right leg had been fractured like dry firewood on the sharp red rock, and a section of her fibula, or calf bone, was missing. Her friends stabilised and splinted the open wound and then picked up the shards of bone that had landed around her and put them into a Ziploc bag. After nine months and countless bouts of surgery to restore her leg, she was still on crutches. Who knows how many years it will take for full rehabilitation. An instant is all it took.

Shaun was next. He had gone to Lysebotn in Norway to jump the huge cliffs that hang over the fjords, and as I bade him farewell I had had a bad feeling about his trip. To be honest, I wasn't sure if I would ever see him again. A month later John called: "Shaun's in intensive care in Stavanger. He's had a cliff-strike on exit point three on Smellvegen." Shaun had slammed into the cliff five unforgiving times on his descent of the 600 metre wall, the force of impact fracturing his skull through a hardy, full-face helmet. The accident cost him the sight in his right eye after a shard of bone from his skull severed the optic nerve. His knee, pelvis and hands were also broken. Shaun is very lucky to be alive. An intensely private man, it was difficult to know the full impact of his accident, but Shaun just couldn't stay away from flying. As he convalesced, he developed a new type of wing-suit that he called a "Sugar Glider" after an Australasian flying squirrel. He started jumping as soon as he could. Two years after his cliff-strike Shaun returned to Norway to confront his ghosts that lurked in the air just beyond those dark cliffs. I joined him there for a flight. From exit point five at Lysebotn we launched ourselves from the cliff top 1000 metres above the grey waters of the fjord. In our Sugar Glider suits we flew away from the wall into the bowl of air, playing in the sky like adolescent birds. We came as close to being swallows as is possible in this human life, revelling in joy, weightlessness, freedom and so much more in our gentle dive down from the heights.

John also had a cliff-strike. A Special Task Force Soldier for the SA Police, he has survived impalement after being speared accidentally by a sharp stick on a hike to a BASE jump, emergency surgery to his spleen, point-blank gunshots to his chest during a SWAT raid, bullets in the Congo, missiles and bombs in Iraq and a ground fall while solo climbing. So, of course, when John had a cliff-strike in Oribi Gorge, Kwa-Zulu-Natal, he survived that too – without injury. John is a real-life Superman or Untouchable. There appears to be nothing on earth that can harm him. He is beyond tough. I don't know what these narrow escapes have cost him, and he wouldn't tell me anyway, even if I asked. John still jumps although none of us see much of him anymore.

And now it was Karl.

My headlight beam reflected a flash of Karl's canopy draped haphazardly over the bushes. He lay in carefully controlled pain on a small incline above the final 200-metre drop to the bottom of Africa Amphitheatre. I hate to see my friends hurt, but I had to banter light-heartedly with him. "That was a spectacular tumble you took there, my lad. I'm sorry we took so long to get here." He was in a lot of pain and he shouted in agony as Moose and I moved him to a safer place away from the edge of the cliff. We gave him some water and tried to make him more comfortable. Hours earlier, just after he'd crashed, Karl had called his girlfriend, Adele Barclay, to tell her that something had "come up" and that he would be late for dinner. Then he called us for help, but that is his nature, always calm and controlled. All he said when we finally reached him was "I really appreciate you coming to get me", as if it were a choice whether we came or not.

Karl had jumped in exactly the same way he had done so many hundreds of times before, only this time his canopy opened facing directly into the mountain. He tried to turn away but struck the cliff before the turn could be completed. After that he became a defence-less rag doll, suspended under a twisted and collapsed parachute that was uncontrollable. He bounced down from ledge to ledge, breaking bones with each impact, fracturing his arm, pelvis and ribs. It could have been a lot worse.

Dr Rik de Decker arrived shortly after Moose and I with the High Angle Rescue Team, and while we waited for the helicopter, the mor-phine that he shot into Karl's arm subdued his pain, along with the last illusions about BASE jumping that lingered in all of our minds. The rescue team strapped him into a stretcher and within the hour an Air Force Oryx helicopter flew in and dropped a long line cable. We clipped Karl into the line and they hoisted him up. Then, while the chopper hovered improbably with rotor blades blurring just metres from the cliff face, the line was dropped again, and, like a scene from a James Bond movie, we were all winched up through the dark night on a thin steel cable into the helicopter and safety.

The empty echoes of so many hospital wards will probably return to haunt us all in the future, in some form or another. My knees hurt when the weather turns. Shaun has adapted to life with one eye very well, but it will frustrate him for the rest of his life. Karl might have difficulty turning doorknobs when he gets older and arthritis sets in, and Lisa will eventually heal and walk unaided, but it's been a long journey. The way I feel about BASE jumping is very different now.

Luck, chance and fate live in a small grey area on the other side of the cliff edge. It's a place where, after you have thrown your pilot chute and caution to the wind and are falling through the trapdoor waiting for your canopy to open, there is nothing more you can do. You might have done everything exactly right, in the same way as all your previous jumps, but this time random probability sends you into the cliff and into hospital, instead of on a beautiful three-minute flight down to the road and a beer with your friends. The more jumps you do, the greater the likelihood of a cliff-strike. We can escape for a while, but it will catch up with you, as the law of averages in this high-stakes game comes into play.

Was it worth it? The lives and bodies we've permanently altered? I suppose the pursuit of danger held an element of self-expression for all of us at the time, a way to find meaning in our lives. But now, when I look at my small children and their perfect little bodies, BASE jumping no longer makes sense. I got off lightly; we all did, because we're still alive, and although I still jump, it's very different now. My passion and intensity have gone, evaporated, like the muffled mental fog of an anaesthesia that has long since worn off. If I do it now, it's simply because I really want to.

On the first anniversary of his accident, Karl climbed up to the small ledge where he had broken himself and sent me a text message on my cell phone: "Standing on the spot where I nearly came to grief exactly one year ago today. Thanks to good friends I'll live to bore my grandchildren with the story. May I never have to return the favour." It was the General's way of saying thank you in his own tightly controlled manner. Karl hasn't BASE jumped since, and probably never will again, because, like most of us, he's moved on to different things. I'm really glad that he'll be able to tell his grandchildren the story. And it's one favour I never want returned from him.

The dream of flying hasn't faded for any of us though. The bird people have simply moved on to different forms of flight. After nearly a year in hospital, Lisa learned how to fly helicopters during her convalescence and she now walks free of her crutches, with her leg strapped into a stiff brace and a barely discernible limp. Shaun operates a skydiving centre in Plettenberg Bay after earning his pilot's licence, and he flies every day. After his accident, Karl turned his life around completely: he quit deep-sea diving and married his girlfriend Adele. He still skydives, flies air planes, and is in the process of opening a new skydiving centre near Ceres. And John, our Rasputin of BASE jumping, moved to Texas in the USA from where he still does "security" tours to Iraq, and in between he BASE jumps every now and then off the big antennae of Florida. Moose quit BASE jumping altogether, before he too became a statistic, and his passion has become cross-country paragliding.

What is it about our yearning to fly like birds that makes it worth the trauma, heartache and pain that we've endured? It's because bird people simply love to fly. It gives us glorious freedom to soar above our own given element, and nothing makes us feel as intently alive.

Imagine this: some time ago, Karl, Shaun and I skydived from a small Cessna six kilometres above the earth, twice as high as our normal jumping altitude. We were so high above the Swartland wheat fields that the plane struggled to climb in the thin air and inside we had to take turns sucking on a bottle of oxygen. In the cramped interior we had to kneel to zip up our suits and adjust our gear. It was the last jump of the day and the sun was a huge red orb hovering over the sea to the west, while far below us the mountains were inky blue in shadow where the sun had already set. The air around us was like milk as the approaching night slowly leached colour from the sky. When the GPS told us we were seven kilometres from the drop zone we opened the door to a frigid blast of air. We all touched hands and then we dived out into space. My heart exploded with pleasure: I was flying again.

We opened the wings of our wingsuits and flew towards the dark mountains, close to each other, like a flock of human birds migrating towards a spiritual place that we are never destined to reach. The air became thicker, darker and denser the lower we flew. We passed over the dark mountains and the road down the Piekenierskloof Pass and into the deep purple shadow of the Citrusdal valley. We flew and flew and flew, coming as close to being birds as we ever could, until, like the mortals we really are, we ran out of time and altitude. With 800 metres left above the ground we all veered off in different directions and opened our parachutes, gliding in to land on the dusty field next to the airstrip. We gathered our deflating canopies, unzipped our wings and walked back to the hangar in the settling gloom.

For a short while we had been eagles, swallows, swifts, griffins, or even small grey pigeons playing in a world we can never inhabit. All of us had found a different kind of freedom, if only for a short while, and that's what makes it worthwhile in the end.

Adventure is a commitment made by the entire being,
and can search our depths to bring out the best, most
human qualities which remain in us. When the
pack of cards has not been rigged so we win
every time, then the game is real, and we
find surprise, imagination, enthusiasm
to succeed and the possibility of failure.

WALTER BONATTI, 1930

A letter from Alaska to Charlotte (and to myself)

How could you have known what it was like in Alaska? Even though I'd been there many times before, the weather was more unsettled than I'd ever seen it. It had snowed six metres in the last two weeks and it was unusually cold. I ran my finger across my mental map of the world, from the scruffy, log-cabined Alaskan outpost of Talkeetna diagonally down to Cape Town, on the other side of the world. It was sunny there, I'm sure, under that cobalt blue African sky, but it was raining in Talkeetna and we waited for four days under ground-level clouds. You must have received the hurried postcard I sent you saying that we'd decided to go into the Ruth Gorge and climb the Ghost Wall on the Eye Tooth. There was a big unclimbed line on the southeast face that we wanted to do. I wrote it in five minutes because Paul, our pilot, was yelling at us to hurry and gear up because a window had appeared in the storm-swollen skies and he wanted to fly us in immediately.

When Paul landed us on the Coffee Glacier in his tinny Cessna it must have been just about the time you went to bed in Cape Town. You were probably already sleeping but we were wide awake as the plane took off and left the two of us alone on that empty glacier. It had taken us 45 minutes to fly in and it would take at least two weeks to walk out if we needed to, over glaciers and rivers, tundra and marshes, through grizzly bear country. But we didn't want to walk out, not just then anyway. As the last faint drone from the plane subsided into a drenching silence, a panic washed over me and I turned instinctively and looked up at the wall eight kilometres away. I felt diminutive and alone in that inhospitable white world and I tried to ignore the despair and be a big brave mountain climber as we set up our tent. After a while the sense of isolation did ease, but let me tell you, that initial absolute silence is eerie and unsettling, especially with the Ghost Wall looming up there, reminding us of why we had come. Suddenly there was no one to rely on but ourselves.

Try to imagine what the Eye Tooth looks like. It's a steep, nasty prehistoric-looking behemoth, dripping sharp rock and veins of ice in its 1200-metre vertical plunge from the summit to the glacier below. And of course it's in the middle of nowhere, tucked tightly into the folds of the Alaska Range. No one goes there.

The weather was quite bad and it snowed every day, but still we hauled loads for three days, ferrying all the equipment and food we needed for the climb up to the base of the cliff. Then we climbed the first three pitches in miserable weather and fixed our ropes down the wall to give us a jumpstart for our ascent push.

Did I talk to you about Steve Swenson? You'll meet him one day and I know you'll like him. Steve is a good partner because, like me, he never gives up. And he's always willing to do the nasty stuff (the things I always have to do). It's really nice to have someone with whom to share the burdens. I've known him for a while, running into him at the gym and at the crag, but this was the first time that we had actually climbed together. At first I was nervous because of the stories and legends that preceded him, you know, the ultimate Himalayan man, Everest and K2 without oxygen, lungs on legs and all that. But as time went on and I got to know him better, I saw past the movie star good looks, past the responsible civil engineer, past the fiery determination that's brought him success on the big peaks and I saw someone who simply loves climbing and being in the mountains. Somehow we clicked because we're both strong and capable and we climbed for the same reasons.

After all that ferrying it snowed harder for four days straight and we holed up in our base camp tent reading, writing. And I thought of you. You would probably think that it would be hard to spend four days cooped up with someone inside a tent, but you know, time passes remarkably quickly. I had brought a duffel bag full of books from that second-hand bookstore on University Avenue in Seattle. (Remember we went there once, that bohemian treasure trove of musty-smelling books piled high from floor to ceiling?) And we would read for hours and then we would talk about anything and everything. When we got tired we would sleep, sometimes for 15 hours straight, like puppies all curled up and content in our down sleeping bags as the snow fell thick and heavy onto the tent.

On the fifth day it cleared and we were able to get back on the rock and continue from where we'd hung our ropes. I lead a pitch that was really satisfying climbing. For once the rock wasn't terrible and the gear was good. The sun came out and it was warm, not like in Africa, but warm enough that I could climb in a pile jacket without the suffocating, waterproof Gore-Tex shell that had become my standard armour against the weather. When I reached the end of the rope, there was just a blank featureless wall, without so much as a foot ledge to stand on. I reached up as far as I could and drilled two expansion bolts into the rock for my anchors. And there I hung, suspended like a fly in the middle of a dead vertical rock face, 500 metres above the ground.

Can you possibly imagine what it was like to hang on that belay for the next nine hours while Steve led the pitch above? As I hung in my harness, with my feet in loops, I felt the cold start to creep in at my feet and slink steadily upwards. There was nothing I could do to stem it and slowly it began to freeze me immobile. I did try to fight it. I stood up and hung back in my harness over and over, and kicked my boots and swung my arms and tried to stop the shivering. I got to know all of the features and micro crystals in the rock in front of my face. And I looked at the vista behind me and it was wild. And the whole time I held Steve's ropes in my hands and paid them out slowly as he inched his way upwards, directly above me.

I couldn't move, couldn't leave, because he was up there drilling rivets and standing on hooks on fragile flakes. I watched with eyes glued to the cams he stood on, knowing that if one of them blew he would fall directly on top of me. I had to trust in God, or Allah, or the rock, or the delicate mechanics of the unit that barely held Steve's body weight. The rock wasn't great. It was typical bleached mountain granite, loose and a little fragile. We had to climb slowly and carefully. I retreated into my own world, as the minutes turned into long cold hours that never seemed to end.

When Steve finally reached the end of his lead we rappelled, with exhausted, chilly relief, back down the two rope lengths to our hanging camp and portaledge, which was tucked underneath an over-hang to protect us from falling ice and rock. Imagine the two of us on a suspended stretcher the size of a single bed, sleeping head to toe, cramped and uncomfortable in the middle of a cold mountain wall.

Then imagine us being there for six days. I think it was six days, but I lost count as the days merged and storm after storm pinned us down. We lay there and waited while the wind pounded us and the snow fell in heavy flakes on our flysheet.

Protected from falling ice by the overhang above and safely tied into our climbing harnesses, which we never removed, we mostly lay still and dozed. Each time one of us did move or turn over it would upset the balance of the ledge, which would rock and creak and groan. And we talked and thought about other places. Warmer places. We used our stove, which hung from the lines of our portaledge just inches from my face, to melt water from ice and ate dehydrated meal packs that tasted really good because that was all there was.

Our flysheet, that thin piece of nylon that sheltered us from the Alaskan storms, was yellow and it reminded me of you, a sunflower. There was no mental escape other than thoughts of you and home.

I remembered the two of us lying on the beach in Cape Town, the sun hot on our bodies, but that memory didn't warm me up much, memories never do. So, like silkworms, we lay in that yellow cocoon of ice, coaxing what little heat there was out of damp sleeping bags while ice chips melted and froze on the ledge floor.

When we finally ran out of food and gas we had no choice but to go down, but first I had to jumar back up to our high point where we'd left our ropes and rack using my sliding ascender clamps. We needed the gear to descend. The storm was still raging and our rope had become encased in a five-centimetre mantle of ice. It quickly became a nightmare, being suspended there in an unreal, buffeting world of whirling snow and wind. Inch by meticulous inch, I cleared the ice away with my gloves so the jumar clamps would stick. Hours passed and I wondered how far you could have run with those marathon-fit legs of yours in the time it took me to climb those ropes. Pitches we had climbed days before were frozen into plate ice, long icicles hung off every lip of rock. Our route had been transformed into a bizarre winter wonderland, except there was no wonder, only numbing cold.

How can you have any idea of what it's like to rappel down in sheets of snowy spindrift, feet skating over the black ice of 'verglas'-covered rock? Do you know what it's like to be cold for a week? I mean really cold, without sufficient hot food to fuel your body. I suppose you must have touched your own body sometime during that week. It must have felt good to touch those muscles, sinews and bones. I hadn't touched my body in over a week, buried as it was under many layers of polypropylene, pile and Gore-Tex. It does what it's told, but I just wish it would stop complaining of cold and hunger.

Steve and I certainly hadn't guessed that it would be possible that the snowfield we had crossed could have avalanched, stopping a fortuitous metre short of taking out our skis at the base of the wall. It would have been desperate if we had lost them because we needed them for travelling on the soft snow on the glaciers below. I suppose it was a sign that our fortunes were in hand, but it didn't seem that way.

But back down at base camp I felt human again. Do you remember I told you my three rules of alpinism? We were hard up against Number 2, Never Give Up, as we waited for three days more while it continued to snow, and we had plenty of time to discuss why we had gotten spanked. Both of us knew we had to go up there again.

It was a Wednesday when it cleared, the second clear day we had had in three weeks, a fine blue bird day. We reclimbed the first pitches and jumarred up our ropes to the portaledge before the sun reached the top of the wall, sending ice bombarding down. As we pulled our ropes up to the high point, the wind started up again, blustering cross-hatched, ominous looking mare's-tail clouds across the southern sky.

I led a diagonal grey pitch up to a ledge that we had named the spider ledge, because it looked like a white spider had fallen out of the sky and landed there, its legs spilling over the edge. To get there I needed to pendulum across the face, so I started running back and forth across the wall until I gained enough momentum to make a swing for the ledge. I just made it at the end of my rope.

Steve had started up the next lead, an arching corner of hollow sounding rock, when we heard the hum of the Cessna. It was Paul flying by to check on us. One of the passes he made was less than 30 metres away. He was so close I could see his teeth as he smiled behind the sunglasses and earmuffs. His plane made a radical bank and flew off down the Coffee Glacier, pretty soon becoming a speck in the distant sky. He would be in Talkeetna in less than an hour. Silence and that profound sense of isolation returned, leaving just the two of us high and alone on that big alpine face.

I imagined you walking on flat earth. Two legs walking. It seems so simple and elementary, but you think about simple walking a lot when you're hanging from the side of a wall. You're always clipped in, always hanging. It becomes almost normal. The two planes, the horizontal and the vertical, are like two different planets. That's why I'm telling you all of this, because our world was so radically different from yours.

I finished cleaning the gear from Steve's pitch at midnight (there is no darkness in an Alaskan springtime, remember?), and we rappelled back down to our portaledge after a 22-hour day. Then the weather shut down again. Two more days of storm and snow kept us in our yellow sunflower. I found it hard to disassociate myself and think of you during these two days. I don't know why, but I just lay there and thought of nothing, my mind a blank.

On the third day a thickly veiled sun came out as a dark black front hung over Mount Foraker. We knew we were going to get nailed, but we packed the ledge to move up anyway. Maybe we were too keen, but I think it was more like we were really trying.

I had just jumarred back up to the spider ledge, when a barrage of ice fell without warning, narrowly missing me, plummeting past the spot where I'd been standing a few minutes before.

Steve wasn't so lucky. He was directly below and got hit. All I heard was his shouting and I knew.

Did I tell you about the strange and disconcerting intuition that came over me on that Wednesday afternoon while I was belaying, just before Paul flew past us? I had a flashing image of me lowering Steve down the wall. Don't ask me why or how, but I knew. Perhaps it was a seventh mountain sense. I only knew now that I had known this would happen, but I suppose that's why it's called intuition. Now it was up to me to get us out of there.

I rappelled down to Steve to find that his shoulder had been broken, crushed by the falling ice. You, my good doctor, would have known how bad his injury was, but all I could see was that he was in agony. The game was over. We had to go down. I jumarred back up the rope to collect the portaledge, a sleeping bag and a fistful of Ibuprofen tablets and then I lowered and rappelled Steve back to the hanging bivouac site we had left a few hours previously. He could use one arm and he was able to clip himself into the anchors at the end of each rope length after I lowered him down. I set up the portaledge and eased Steve into his sleeping bag. He's a tough guy, but I could see that he was in a lot of pain.

By now the next storm was upon us. This one was warmer than the last and it plastered the wall with horizontal driving slush, soaking me instantly as I jumarred back up the ropes to retrieve our gear. As I struggled to clear the mantle of ice coating the rope, it was like an action replay of two weeks previously. This time it took me eight hours to reach our high point and lower all of our gear back down; I know because I looked at my watch when I reached the ledge, soaked, freezing and shivering uncontrollably. You know how cold you get surfing in the Atlantic? Imagine spending the night out there in the sea on your surfboard. It felt like that during that horrible night on the portaledge in a sodden sleeping bag. All the while Steve lay grimly silent with his broken shoulder. We were both miserable; Steve's shoulder blade felt like the sharp edge of an Aiguille in Chamonix, France, and the whole of his back had bruised purple and yellow into a Rorschach ink-blot. I'd immobilised his arm by strapping it tightly to his torso with thermal clothing and some climbing slings. Steve didn't say much. He just sat there and silently controlled the pain. I'd also fashioned a backrest out of slings and he slept sitting up because it hurt too much to lie down in such a cramped space. And all the while my mind was racing about how I was going to get down with a disabled partner and a ton of gear.

It snowed hard that night and in the morning the whole wall was plastered white with snow. Then it warmed up and the mountain face became a hazardous water world with barrages of ice crashing through thick wet snowflakes as the sun melted the ice's grip on the rock. It was like being at war with the elements, pinned under heavy fire. I won't describe the descent because it was hellish, but we did it because we had to. I suppose we rally ourselves when we have no choice. I jettisoned the haulbags packed with all our bivouac gear straight off the cliff and they fell clear of the rock for long seconds before bouncing once off the snowfield directly below and coming to a slithering stop on the glacier. We descended straight down the rocks next to the snowfield because Steve couldn't down climb on snow with one arm, and we left most of our piton rack behind in a freezing maelstrom of snow, wind and water.

But we did get down, safely, back onto the glacier and then we skied down in a whiteout, dragging haulbags in zero visibility. Steve skied one-handed, but then we all know that he is as tough as they come.

We reached base camp late that night and changed into dry clothes, put our hands around steaming mugs of tea and tried our best to forget the previous six days, as if they had been some dislocated nightmare. Steve took some Codeine pills and fell into a drugged sleep, pain-free for the first time in days. We radioed for Paul to come and collect us, but it was four long days before the weather cleared enough for him fly in, land and pick us up. Steve lay very still for those four days, because the slightest bump or sudden movement made him yelp and we both turned our thoughts to home and to the future.

I could tell you about peering out of the little Cessna windows as we flew out, staring down at the reflected light on the tundra marshes and lakes. They look like translucent mercury as the veiled reflection of the sun on the plane's wing passed briefly overhead. I could also tell you about the budding green leaves on the birch trees in Talkeetna, or the odd sensation of walking on dry land, away from snow and ice and rock. But strangest of all, I have to tell you, was the noise, of cars and telephones and people and connectivity, and the noise in my ears after a glass of Glenlivet single-malt Scotch whisky.

But I couldn't tell you any of this when you walked off the plane and into my arms back in Seattle a week later. It didn't matter because you were there and I didn't want to think about freezing snow and falling ice while the sun warmed our bodies in the grass beside the lake. When we swam in the cool water or climbed on warm rock at the crag, it all seemed unimportant and so distantly far away. It's only now that I need to tell you how we tried and how severely we were beaten by the weather. Sometimes it's like that, you try and try and try and you still don't get there.

Perhaps this isn't even a letter to you, but one written to myself to say that it's OK to try and OK to fail, as long as you give your best.

Sometimes you have to tell yourself that.

Somewhere

I walk alone now – veiled in imaginings
A difference lies out there – somewhere
Beyond the heat and the trembling of humanity,
Beyond the faceless.

Somewhere: continuity exists
Intricate subtleties, webbed connections.

Something lies outside here
I can sense its patterns
Turn within me
A fluttering of life like an unborn child.

Somewhere: something is missing,
Out of place.

Somewhere: a Catherine Wheel of fire
Splutters and dies.

Somewhere: 10 000 miles away a candle burns
For eternity or the dead.

Somewhere: in the silence
I am missing you.

AdK

J'aime celui qe reve l'impossible.
I love the one who dreams of the impossible.

JOHANN WOLFGANG VON GOETHE, 1749–1832

Between Desert and Sky

The truck stopped in a swirling cloud of dust and the engine clicked in the sudden silence. Around us the Southern Saharan desert stretched flat and endless, so flat that the earth seemed to curve downwards at the edges. Dust settled on us, thick enough to taste and bitter enough to want to drink it away. It was a dry heat and blisteringly hot. I was already thirsty and we'd only just arrived.

We had travelled around the world to reach this desolate and desperate spot in the middle of Mali, in the remote northwest corner of Africa, where, as if by some bizarre geological mishap, the five spires of La Main de Fatima shot skywards for 600 metres straight out of the dusty plain.

Standing below them, the slender fingers of solid quartzite looked wickedly steep and unsettlingly out of place.

We jumped off the truck and I immediately saw the line we would climb. A glance at Ed February, my oldest friend and climbing partner, and I saw his eyes glued to the same thing. It was obvious: Kaga Tondo, the thinnest of the spires, had a clean corner that split sun and shade like the vertical corner of a skyscraper.

"Think it'll go?"

"Dunno. Looks amazing though."

We were here because we wanted to free-climb something big, something really big, in Africa. It had taken a lot of organisation, planning, funding and hectic travel to get here. And the prize route looked totally impossible.

As we unloaded our gear people began to slink up out of the desert. Barefoot, large-eyed and malnourished, the local villagers drew up and settled silently onto their haunches to watch us set up our tents among the boulders below the spires. It wasn't long before we had a group of about 40 Malians all dressed in rags squatting in the dust in our camp, vacant eyes impassively following every move we made. That afternoon we made acquaintance with a big man named Djenare and agreed that he would act as guardian of our camp, cook, and most importantly, water collector. The closest drinkable water was at a well-point six kilometres away. As the late afternoon sun blistered the sky white with heat, Ed and I melted and it soon became apparent that the heat, rather than the climbing, would be a major factor on any route we climbed. It was the middle of winter and the temperature was 48 degrees Celsius.

The rest of the lads arrived the next day on a clapped-out West African bus after a nerve-jarring Malian travel experience that could best be described as character-building, and that included roadblocks, AK47-toting soldiers, bribe-seeking officials, overcrowding and mechanical breakdowns. Our team now included the charismatic American big wall climber and cowboy, Todd Skinner, Canadian Scott Milton, Ed and me. Our fifth climbing team member, Paul Piana, was still somewhere in Europe trying to arrange a Malian visa and nobody knew when or whether he would arrive. Skinner had arranged funding at the very last minute from American Adventure Network Television, an independent subsidiary of ESPN, and he brought along American film crew Bill Hatcher, Peter Mallermo and Bob Model. Ed and I had initiated the trip and we were the token Africans, although Mali was as foreign to us as the moon.

It was a diverse group but a strong team and we had brought lots of power with us: three drills with solar panels to charge the batteries,

300 bolts, over a kilometre of fixed rope, and a mountain of big wall gear. We were fairly confident of climbing a good free route, although after several hours of scanning the arête, a knife-like ridge of rock that formed Kaga Tondo's spine, with binoculars, there were still sections that looked impassable and blank despite our hopeful scrutiny.

Todd grinned at the challenge. He was no stranger to big blank walls. A burly, powerful all-American guy, his classic approach to a climb like this was to barge right in using muscle, brute force and determination, like taming a wild horse on his ranch in Wyoming. Just march in, beat it down and you'll get it in the end. This technique had worked well for him and Paul, his long-time climbing partner, on the first free ascent of the Salathe wall in Yosemite, USA, where they spent 30 remarkable days free-climbing every pitch in an impressive frenzy of pure, unaided climbing. They'd done the same on other hard walls the world over, including the legendary Nameless Tower in Pakistan.

Todd was an inveterate believer in free-climbing: climbing up a cliff under his own power using the ropes only for protection against falling, instead of hanging off his gear and using it as a direct aid to his climbing. Todd then controversially took things one step further by bringing 'sport climbing' to the big walls. Sport climbing is when strong, bombproof expansion bolts are drilled into the rock for protection, allowing climbers to take difficult moves to unimaginable gymnastic levels without worrying about whether their protection gear will hold their weight if they take a fall. Sport climbing spread like wildfire in the late 1980s on the smaller cliffs of the world and Todd was one of the first to consistently apply this ethic to the big walls. Slowly but surely, climbers around the world began to take notice of the impressive ascents he kept pulling off and with a little savvy marketing of himself and his exploits, Todd had became one of only a handful of professional climbers worldwide. Scott Milton, on the other hand, was the complete opposite of Todd: a gaunt, skinny and delicate man, he was one of the best sport climbers in the world and it was lovely to watch him climb. He flowed like water; never hesitating or outwardly showing effort. Scott was the epitome of finesse with power to spare.

In the end we decided to do a recce by climbing up to the top of the spire and stringing a line of rope down our route so that we could have a close look at it and see if it were climbable. It sounded simple, but even that ended up becoming a major endeavour because there were three existing routes up the spire: two going up the back and one going up the side face to the right of our line, and all three were hard adventures in themselves. We were faced with a lot of work just to determine whether or not our route was even possible.

Todd and Scott set off to climb one of the routes up the back of the tower. We had a great plan: they were going to climb up and over the top and then fix ropes down the upper half of our route, while Ed and I were to climb halfway up the existing route to the right, pendulum across the face, and then fix ropes down the lower half. The theory was impeccable, but it turned into a minor epic. We underestimated the difficulty of the introductory climbs and the logistics needed to haul up the vast amounts of gear we needed. We ended up taking twice as long as we'd predicted with the result that Ed and I found ourselves plastered onto a small pedestal halfway up our new route, in the pitch dark, while our headlamps were stashed safely, and uselessly, in our packs on the ground, 250 metres below. Spiderman might have enjoyed being there 70 storeys above the desert in the middle of the night, but we didn't. From somewhere in the darkness above us, Todd and Scott's voices floated down as they had a quiet struggle of their own.

It was time to get off the rock and down to safety. "Be careful, kid," said Ed into the inky blackness as I rappelled down and tied our two extra ropes together, passing the knots totally by feel.

Completely blind and hanging sickeningly far from the ground, my senses were electric. The slightest mistake could send me into a horrifying plunge. The rappel that took me to the ground was totally free hanging, and, slowly spinning in the darkness, I was beyond grateful to reach solid earth, especially as I had a mere 30 centimetres of rope left to spare. If we'd been any higher I would have been stuck, dangling above ground, jammed hard against the knot on the end of the rope. It was a close call. We just barely got down, but in climbing, just barely is always enough.

But I did swear never again to leave my headlamp behind and I was very relieved when Ed dropped lightly and safely onto the sand beside me. "Fuckin' hell, that was an epic", was all he said. We still had some Wild Turkey whiskey left, so we both headed down to calm our shaking nerves.

The next day we jumared back up the ropes we had strung down the rock to inspect the route in daylight. Three sections looked desperately hard and one part in particular, high on the sheer edge, surmounted a blank wall that looked almost unclimbable. Ed named this pitch "Weetbix", because he struggled to articulate 8C+, which is pronounced '*weet see plus*' in French, which was the hardest grade in the world at the time. Ed never was very good with languages.

For 16 days we worked on the route, still not entirely convinced we would be able to free-climb it. A rock tossed from the top fell clear for half a kilometre of sheer vertical rock before it hit the ground. It was dizzyingly high and all of us felt the exposure as we hung on centimetre thick strands of rope gawking at the prospect of desperately hard climbing. To give ourselves the best chance to free-climb this immaculate line, we needed to prepare the route meticulously and so we jumared, cleaning off loose bits of rock, drilling bolts, and top roping pitches, slowly breaking the route down into manageable chunks. Because of the searing heat, which relentlessly bombarded us day after day, we shifted our days around to start climbing at two in the afternoon when the wall had fallen into shade and continuing until well after midnight in the relatively cool 30-degree night-time temperatures.

It was brutally strenuous. I'd feel weak and hungry by the time I'd jumared the 500 interminable metres to the top of the ropes, and then we still had hard work to do up there. I was constantly thirsty, no matter how much lukewarm water I drank.

As incipient dehydration and our horrible diet, which wasn't enough to sustain our athletic energy output, took its toll, we slowly began to waste. In addition, Ed and I had done a rather dire job of food shopping when we'd purchased our staple food supplies on our journey in from a mud-walled shop in the nearest town, 500 kilometres away. In Mali there are no supermarkets, just little shops run by merchants.

Blinking in the gloom of the shop's interior I'd looked around and seen only rice, biscuits and tinned food on the sparse shelves and I realised then we were going to be hungry. We selected what we thought was enough food. It made a very small, sorry pile on the dirt floor. Ed turned to me and famously asked: "Do you think that's enough food to feed eight people over three weeks?" Ed's question became a standing joke as our food supplies dwindled. I'd asked the shopkeeper to double everything in the pile, but still it wasn't enough. We lived on rice, canned vegetables and tomato sauce and by the time we left a lonely tin of peas was all that remained.

Our diet was terrible and Djenare's cooking skills were appalling. He cooked soggy rice with canned vegetables and soggy rice with canned tuna, and that was it. For breakfast we ate dry biscuits, and, thankfully for us, he didn't have to cook those. We had brought some energy bars with us but they were soon eaten. And still the Malian villagers continued to watch. There were always at least 20 pairs of eyes glued to our every move: as we slept, ate, read, shaved, sorted gear, or pottered with any of the tiny chores that make up expedition life.

Our living environment was filthy and we all started to get sick. Ed came down with malaria from a mosquito that had bitten him in Bamako on the day we arrived and he lay feverish and sick in his sleeping bag in the 50-degree heat. Luckily for us, two Dutch Peace Corps workers, who happened to be driving by, recognised his symptoms. They dosed him with Fansidar, a powerful anti malarial drug that killed the malaria, but which left Ed as weak as a kitten afterwards. Skinner caught a nasty nose infection that had him sneezing trails of green slime, and the whole camera crew came down with violent diarrhoea from drinking contaminated water at a muddy pond, despite having filtered it with their high-tech American water pump. We began to lose momentum and progress started to falter.

Just as it seemed that things could not get worse, the Harmattan winds started up, blowing hot, dry and dusty off the Northern Sahara. The Harmattan is the colloquial name for a savage wind that turns the sky murky with dust, creating a haze that can block the sun and costs airlines millions in flight diversions and cancellations. When the Harmattan really blows, it can drive sand and dust clear across the Atlantic to South America. It deposited fine sand everywhere, into our eyes, our teeth, our food, our tents, everywhere. There was nowhere for us to escape the relentless wind. Periodically Tuareg camel caravans passed our camp, emerging from the dust with their iconic blue turbans wound tightly around their heads until only their eyes were visible, and even the camels have special veiled eyelids that protect them from the blowing sand. The channelling effect created by the towers accelerated the winds to 100 kilometres per hour or more, and it became physically impossible to climb some of the arête pitches because we would have been blown off the rock by violent gusts. And no matter how hard we tightened down our line of fixed ropes against the wind, they still kept abrading against sharp edges of rock, making jumaring up the ropes a spine-chilling nightmare for the first man up, because he wouldn't know if the rope would break under his weight or not. Every time we encountered an abrasion we'd tie it in a knot, and after a while there were more knots than rope. It seemed as if we were being tested to the maximum in the harsh desert conditions.

A little over two weeks after arriving, Christmas rolled in. We decided to take a rest day. Our spirits were particularly low as we sat on a rock hot enough to fry an egg and mournfully contemplated our Christmas dinner, an emaciated and pathetically bleating goat that was clearly as unhappy as we were. While Djenare sharpened his knife blade on our rock before cutting its throat, a truck pulled up and out hopped Paul Piana. He was fresh and strong and he had brought a bag full of power bars and food from Europe. Our Christmas cheer picked up considerably as we added Spanish fish and crackers to our buffet of stringy goat and soggy rice eaten in the dirt. All the same, I have had better Christmases.

Paul's arrival gave a welcome boost to our flagging energies. During the next few days we finished all the bolting and preparation for the climb, which we had split into 13 magnificent, airy pitches. While we had been working up there we had rehearsed free-climbing all of the pitches except Weetbix, which Scott had worked on extensively, but hadn't yet managed to free-climb, and the route was nearly fully prepared. We had spent weeks on the route and had climbed sections of it many times over, but ethically we couldn't claim it as a proper ascent until we free-climbed it continuously from bottom to top in one push. Between the desperately hard climbing and the heat, we figured we would probably need to spend several nights on the wall. The only ledge big enough to accommodate us all was near the top, but all the rest of the climb was sheer, vertical rock and for that we would need portaledges; aluminium-framed hanging stretchers we could camp on. And so, late one afternoon, we started our big push, free-climbing up to a big overhang under which we set up a hanging camp, intending to free-climb to the summit the next day.

It was a glorious, mild evening. Since there were five of us, we erected two double portaledges, one for Todd and Ed, another for Scott and Paul, and a single one for me. Since a double 'ledge is about the size of a single bed, and a single is like trying to sleep on a windowsill, accommodation was rather cramped, but we were all in high spirits as we pulled out a big pot of Djenare's soggy rice and vegetables for dinner.

But later that evening a violent, raging Harmattan wind blew in and savaged our carefully laid plans, giving us a hellish night that none of us will ever forget. As the wind hammered and buffeted our portaledges, throwing us backwards and forwards, we hung on to the aluminium frames for dear life. Not one of us slept. We were all on edge, not sure if our 'ledges could withstand the howling wind or if they would break. We held on through the long dark hours expecting the frames to snap or the fabric to tear at any second, sending us tumbling into the black, wind-blasted void. It was a wild, wild ride and, as Todd put it later, "Quite the Rodeo". Dawn finally broke and we were all relieved. The wind hadn't abated at all, but at least we could see. Folding the portaledges was a nightmare and we struggled to get down with our haulbags swinging like wild animals below us. Back down on the ground, I felt like I had been mugged.

But after a day of rest down in the camp, night fell, bringing a full moon and a brief window of calm between wind and heat, And we took full advantage of it by reclimbing the route, going up pitch after pitch of unrelentingly vertical and sustained climbing. The next day we arrived at the Weetbix pitch in the late afternoon. It was the last crucial section we needed to overcome and Scott still hadn't managed to free-climb it yet. Five pairs of eyes fixed, with burning intensity, on Scott's right hand as he launched a crux dyno on the last move of the pitch. If he could get this right we were home and dry. It stuck, and the route was free. All we had to do now was finish pitches we'd rehearsed.

After a night on the only ledge on the wall, dawn crept over the desert and up the spire to where we were bivouacked, two pitches beneath the top. The morning light was veiled and murky in a dust-filled sky and it felt surreal as we climbed the final two rope lengths and pulled onto the summit of Kaga Tondo. Below, in ropes and gear, was our testimony to the 21 days of hard effort. The summit was just big enough for the five of us to sit there, all shell-shocked and sick, pinned on our eyrie between desert and sky. We stayed just long enough for some summit pictures and then Todd said: "OK, we're done here, let's blow outta town." The hardest big wall free climb in Africa was done.

Up on the summit I smiled for the camera, but I didn't feel good. In fact I felt awful. There was a weird ache in my head and my leg had begun to swell up as the first stages of septicaemia set in. I needed to descend. Quickly. Two days earlier I had slipped while carrying portaledges down the hill and banged my shin. Normally such a minor cut would have been innocuous, but not in Mali. We were living in dirt, goat and camel shit, dust and flies. Nothing was clean. My leg had quickly become infected. I managed to rappel down the long lengths of ropes and I made it to camp before passing out, flattened by microbacteria. The true remoteness of our position hit home as the others stripped the fixed ropes and descended with all of the gear. I lay in the dust and watched my leg swell up like a balloon, sending angry red tracers marching under the skin up my leg, past my groin and up my stomach. And I wondered, anxiously, in between bouts of unconsciousness, whether I would die when they reached my heart. Ed evacuated me to the nearest hospital in Bamako 1600 kilometres away in a marathon, and very costly 30-hour bus and taxi ride. I don't remember much of the journey, but I do remember passing through many roadblocks, as the driver explained "*Cassé le jamb*" (broken leg) and the soldiers waved us through with a "*Bon santé*" (good health). In Bamako, Ed found a decent French-run UN clinic and persuaded them to treat me even though I wasn't French. He then went out and bought all the giant sterile syringes I needed, together with massive doses of penicillin, which they then injected into me three times a day. Ed's tenacity and unfailing assistance saved me from a very serious medical emergency. All it took was a tiny little cut in the middle of the desert to threaten my life. I realised how naïve we had been: our first-aid kit consisted of Asprin, band-aids and not much else, and was in no way appropriate for our isolation.

In the end it took four months for my leg to heal. It didn't stop me travelling though. I saw doctors in four countries, and it was only when Charles Edelstein, a doctor friend of mine in Cape Town, handed me a tub full of powerful antibiotics and said, "Take as many as you can until you puke, and then take one less", that the stubborn West African infection cleared up. It was close, but this time just barely was too close.

We all left Mali sobered by the experience and acutely aware of just how much we had been beaten down in the process of climbing Kaga Tondo. It had been unexpectedly hard on a team that was pretty impressively seasoned in expedition hardships. Despite the relentless heat, wind and sickness, and the difficult, taxing climbing environment, we had pulled together as a strong group and we'd spent an arduous month complementing each other's skills and strengths. It was a route all of us will remember for its hard, steep, continuous and complicated climbing on some of the best rock I have ever touched. All we left behind was a line of bolts and a few chalked finger-holds; the only evidence of a superb climb up the side of an incredible spire caught between desert and sky.

A year later I asked Ed, as we were on our way to the wilds of Cameroon, this time with a crate of medical supplies, whether he would ever go back. He didn't even hesitate: "No."

But you never know with these things. Nothing is ever impossible.

Ed

It's late, well past midnight, as Ed and I sit at my kitchen table drinking single-malt Scotch whisky. I'm feeling drunk, but the conversation has reached that stage of clarity and introspection that only comes near the end of a bottle.

Ed and I don't see enough of each other these days because both of us run busy and responsible lives, but when we do it's like slipping into an old pair of jeans; our conversation is comfortable, the banter familiar, and the silences easy.

"You won't believe how much I've needed you," says Ed.

"Nor how much I've needed you," I reply.

In the 25 years that we have been friends, I guess we have needed each other more than we've realised. Our shared history is interlaced like a tangled mess of climbing rope haphazardly uncoiled and thrown to the ground. There is a sinuous continuity to it all, a common thread of mutual trust and respect.

We catch up on each other's lives well into the early hours and I feel happy. Our connection is still strong. Both of us have changed a lot as we've grown older, but we're still friends and that's what really matters.

I first met Ed in 1982 underneath Newlands Bridge in Cape Town, where all the climbers went during the week to hone their fingertips on the rough stone embankments. All I saw was a huge afro and lots of muscles. A few days previously I had attended a slideshow that Ed had given at The Metrople Hotel in Cape Town, and not, as is standard, at the Mountain Club of South Africa because they didn't want to have anything to do with him. I was transfixed with the images of their recent climbing trip to Yosemite in the USA. Pictures of Ed and his friend Greg Lacey climbing the legendary rock faces of El Capitan, The Prow, and The Right Side of The Folly flicked through the darkness and I was transported to a different world.

They became my instant heroes, so when I saw them at the bridge in person they seemed like gods. In reality, Ed was just a fiery young man who smoked Texan plain cigarettes and had a burning passion for climbing. He was also a highly talented climber, 26 at the time and 12 years my senior. Greg walked up to me while I tried to be as nonchalant as a 14-year-old can be. "Hey, youth," he said, "We're going climbing on Saturday. You coming?" Ed's since told me that when he heard that Greg had invited me climbing he wasn't at all keen to have me along, but after a few days climbing together he warmed to me. He says he decided to climb with me after seeing my raw talent and before I killed myself. It wasn't long before we were climbing together all the time.

My parents had divorced when I was 12 and not long after that I started climbing. My alcoholic father was absent during my formative and vulnerable adolescent years. And that's where Ed comes into things. I was a malleable teenager and Ed took me under his wing. He helped to shape me and then he let me fly. Ed was to become part-father, part-benevolent uncle and part-friend.

Ed is a multifaceted man, more so than most people. He is sociable, irascible, voluble and deeply loyal to his friends, but he is also soft hearted and introspective. He has a vulnerable, dark side that he seldom shows in public. At the crag Ed can greet his friends with a crushing bear hug and then loudly tear them to pieces with comic banter, but he can also spend hours tending his garden in silence, alone with his thoughts. Ed loves beer, the icebreaker to all social situations, although nowadays his taste leans more towards good wines and whisky. Even now, in his early fifties, he is small, lean, fit, and finely muscled, and he sports a neatly trimmed Afro haircut and goatee beard, both of which have gone completely grey. He accuses me of being the one who gave him the grey hair by scaring him while we were climbing, but it is just time that has lent him his distinguished professorial look.

Ed is coloured and I am white, but I have never seen him as anything other than Ed, my friend. People have tried to make something of our racial differences, but the truth is that both of us grew up under fairly similar middle-class circumstances. We are both motivated people who make the best of whatever situation we find ourselves in and the question of race always been a non-issue between us. Even so, Ed's experiences growing up were very different to my own. He was marginalised, I wasn't, and shadows of it still remain.

Edmund Carl February was born in 1955, two years after the New Zealand beekeeper Edmund Hillary and Sherpa Tenzing Norgay climbed Mount Everest, becoming the first to stand on the summit, galvanising the world. His parents were excited by that ascent, liked the name Edmund, and, blissfully unaware of any prophecy in it, named their child after the famous mountaineer. Ed's grandmother was Javanese and his surname stems from the month in which one of his ancestors, a slave, was emancipated. His father, Ronald February, was a slight, finely featured schoolteacher and his mother, Helen, worked as a librarian at the University of Cape Town. Ed and his two brothers grew up in the hard-working, middle-class neighbourhood of Wynberg in Cape Town's southern suburbs. Their house was a neat, ordinary, white-washed semidetached cottage adjacent to a park. In all respects it should have been an ordinary childhood, except that this was apartheid South Africa, and nothing was ordinary. The movements of coloured and black people were severely restricted and national parks and game reserves were off limits. So during the summer holidays, Ed's parents loaded the children into their Hillman sedan and took them out of the country to camp and hike in Lesotho, Swaziland, Zimbabwe and Mozambique. These trips instilled in Ed a deep love of nature and of the raw power of Africa that has endured to this day.

After high school Ed enrolled at the University of the Western Cape (UWC), but his studies were doomed from the start. The Soweto uprisings erupted in 1976 and everything went pear-shaped. He took part in some demonstrations against the government and the rigours of apartheid, but the state's martial response with sjamboks and tear gas didn't do it for him. "The first couple of protests, you get caught and beaten up, then you learn to run away." Ed quit UWC in 1977 after walking out of a revisionist history lesson condoning Afrikaner supremacy and moved to Johannesburg to train as an industrial radiographer, learning to use X-rays to test welds in oil refineries and at the Koeberg Nuclear Power Station on the Cape West Coast. Of apartheid Ed says, "I think I'm probably more bitter about it now than I was then. Then it was the system. You didn't go around feeling anything about it, you just dealt with it." His way of dealing with apartheid was to run away to the mountains. "It was a pretty sick society. Climbing was normal."

Ed started climbing early, when he was 14, on Elsie's Peak and Muizenberg Crags with an uncle, Charlie Hankey and friends of his father's, George Ganget, Errol Flint and Brian Brock. Soon Ed was out-climbing his early mentors. By 16 Ed had joined the Cape Province Mountain Club, a climbing organisation that had developed in parallel to the all-white Mountain Club of South Africa (MCSA), and he started to hone his skills on Table Mountain, together with his younger brother, Rodney, and friends Roderick Appollis, Keith Appollis, Brian Saville and Maurice Wyngard. But of the top white climbers of the early seventies, all MCSA members, they couldn't find anyone to climb with them and stretch their capabilities. It was in 1974 that Dave Cheesmond, a visionary white climber who would go on to establish hard new routes in the Canadian Rockies, broke the ice and invited Ed to climb with him. Dave was the man who delivered Ed to the door of South Africa's golden age of climbing, and standing there were his eventual partners and colour-blind friends, Greg and Tienie Versveldt.

Once Ed had taken the teenage me under his wing, I would spend every weekend clambering into the back of his red Datsun bakkie, to be driven off to the crags to climb with him and a group of friends who, by and large, were a good decade older than me. One of the things that strikes Ed as amazing was that my mother relinquished me into the hands of a 'Darkie' in the dark days of apartheid. With her blessing and trust, I would be allowed to head into the hills with Ed for days and weeks at a time. There were places where we couldn't climb because of access problems and racist farmers who wouldn't allow Ed on their land, but we made the best of it and simply climbed elsewhere.

Ed often picked me up after school and we would race off to climb a few routes before dark. I hated school and couldn't relate to anyone there because my interests lay beyond the school walls. But on the few occasions when I did hang out and experiment with my peers, it would be Ed who would come and haul me out of the bushes in a marijuana-induced stupor, revive me and take me home. Ed was the person I looked up to and admired both on the cliffs and off them. It was he who taught me the little-known essentials like how to cook boerewors on a stick and how to open a bottle of beer with a brick.

One morning in the Cedarberg I unzipped Ed's tent at 5.30 to hand him a cup of steaming tea because I was so keen to get going. He opened one bleary eye, looked at me and said, "Fuck off", and then went back to sleep. I was quite put out, so I drank his tea as well as mine and then I leaned against a bluegum tree and sulked for a while. I passed some time bouldering on some nearby rocks, came back and sorted out our gear, and all the while Ed slumbered. Hours later I made him another cup of tea and this time all he said was "Ta." I was insufferable, but he put up with it.

Our passion was to be the first to climb the innumerable unclimbed rock faces in the Western Cape. Together Ed and I must have opened 500 new climbs, possibly more, indelibly printing our partnership onto South African climbing. After a while we stopped counting. There were some days when everything just clicked, when we would climb long routes without needing to say a single word because each simply anticipated the needs of the other. I would be about to ask for the rack of gear and it would already be in Ed's outstretched hand, or he wouldn't need to say "Watch me" on a hard move, because I had already felt the tension coming down the rope and was watching closely.

Ours was a partnership bred of a mutual trust in each other's abilities on the rock, and although our styles of climbing were different, we made a good team. Ed is a naturally conservative climber, bold, but not foolhardy, while I tended to run it out more often. He has a powerful way of climbing, using bulldog-like brute force more often than finesse, and there is very little that can pry him off once he has sunk his hands into a crack. A love of climbing was the central thread to both our lives.

When asked why he climbs, Ed says, "How can I explain that it's pushing one's body to the absolute limits, walking a tightrope between disaster and glory, but treading that very fine line with one's eyes wide open. That's what I enjoy about climbing. Being out there, at the extreme limits of my ability, with a really good reliable partner."

When Ed takes his shirt off it's quite a sight. What you see is an incredible physique with muscles to spare and scars that map a 35-year climbing history like tattoos. Take for instance the arching welt that runs from shoulder blade to hip: a rope burn inflicted when he held Roderick Appollis' fall with a body belay in the early days of his climbing career. Look at the palms of his hands and you'll see rough mottled scar tissue where he burnt them by stopping my rope and saving my life. We were rappelling off the sheer northwest face of Du Toit's Peak one afternoon when one of the ends of my two ropes slid through my braking device and I started tumbling uncontrollably down the cliff. I was facing a 200-metre fall and certain death. Ed saw the ropes whizzing through the anchors and, without thinking, grabbed onto them with his bare hands and held tight. He stopped my fall and burnt his hands, but he didn't let go. It was a close one. All he said was, "You blew it, kid", and then he didn't speak to me for a month afterwards. He was so pissed off that he wouldn't talk about it, but the real reason is that he cared and it was just his way of showing it.

The ugly scar on Ed's foot came from the 30-metre fall he took on Paarl Rock, while we were trying to open a new route late one Sunday afternoon. Strung out, and far above his last protection piece, Ed slipped and plummeted, clipping his heel on a narrow ledge on the way down. That little ledge rearranged all the bones in his foot and

1

This is me where I am most at home, in the mountains where there is no one to show me the way. Welcome to my world.

As soon as I was out of university I headed out to climb
the earth's snowy peaks.

3

Part father-figure, part-mentor, part-friend, Ed and I have been joined together
by a climbing rope for almost as long as I can remember.

5

4

6

7

*Ed is many men: the leading academic, the climber and the happily married man,
equally at home with Nicky in Nepal, on his stoep in the Bo-Kaap or hanging on
the side of Table Mountain.*

The stress before a BASE jump is betrayed by the faces of Karl (left) and Alistair McQueen. Safe landings are always happy times as Karl drops down onto Table Mountain Road in perfect conditions.

OPPOSITE: *Dream St Rose is the name of a test piece on Elsie's Peak, Cape Town. I opened the route 20 years ago and it still feels hard.*

12

13

The only way to learn how to fly a wingsuit is to fly it. The soaring cliffs of Norway's fjords gave Moose and I plenty of airspace to do so.

14

Lower wall, Milner Peak. Three seconds to go till impact. It's time to pull!
It's time … It's time …

15

16

17

18

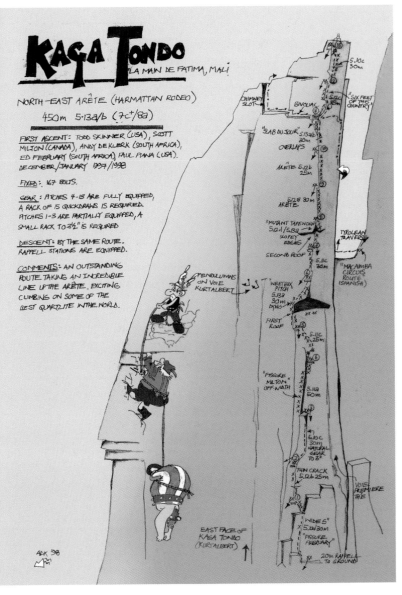

KAGA TONDO
LA MAIN DE FATIMA, MALI

NORTH-EAST ARÊTE (HARMATTAN RODEO)
450m 5.13a/b (7c+/8a)

FIRST ASCENT: TODD SKINNER (USA), SCOTT
MILTON (CANADA), ANDY DE KLERK (SOUTH AFRICA),
ED FEBRUARY (SOUTH AFRICA) PAUL PIANA (USA).
DECEMBER/JANUARY 1997/1998

FIXED: 167 BOLTS.

GEAR: PITCHES 4-13 ARE FULLY EQUIPPED,
A RACK OF 15 QUICKDRAWS IS REQUIRED.
PITCHES 1-3 ARE PARTIALLY EQUIPPED, A
SMALL RACK TO 3½" IS REQUIRED.

DESCENT: BY THE SAME ROUTE.
RAPPELL STATIONS ARE EQUIPPED.

COMMENTS: AN OUTSTANDING
ROUTE TAKING AN INCREDIBLE
LINE UP THE ARÊTE. EXCITING
CLIMBING ON SOME OF THE
BEST QUARTZITE IN THE WORLD.

CHIMNEY SLOT
BIVOUAC
"SIX FEET OF THE COUNTRY"
"SLAB DU JOUR" 5.13a/b 30m
OVERLAPS
ARÊTE 5.12b 25m
5.12b 30m ARÊTE
TYROLEAN TRAVERSE
"MUTANT TAPEWORM" 5.12a/5.13a SLOPEY EDGES
SECOND ROOF
5.11c 30m
5.10c 30m
"MACAMBA CIRCUS ROUTE" (SPANISH)
PENDULUMS ON VOIE KURT ALBERT
"WEETBIX PITCH" 5.13a 30m DYNO"
FIRST ROOF
5.11c 25m
"FISSURE MILTON" OFF-WIDTH
5.11a 60m
5.10c 30m NATURAL GEAR TO 3"
THIN CRACK 5.12b 25m
VOIE PREMIERE THE
"WIDE 5" 5.10c 30m
"FISSURE FEBRUARY"
20m RAPPEL TO GROUND

EAST FACE OF KAGA TONDO (KURT ALBERT)

ADK '98

*Christmas in Mali was pretty ropey, despite our cook Djenare's efforts to be festive.
But the climbing was good. We climbed the line of light and shadow on Kaga Tondo,
the thinnest spire on the left.*

Big wall climbing is physical, strenuous and technical. Cowboy Todd Skinner tackled Mali's steep rock like he'd tackle a steer back home in Wyoming. (In the end Todd would die on a big wall in Yosemite when his equipment failed in 2006 and he fell 200 metres).

20

21

22

23

24

25

Kaga Tondo's summit: (left to right)
Scott Milton, Todd Skinner, myself and
Paul Piana with Ed in front. By this time
a simple scratch I'd got on the ground was
quickly becoming life-threatening, and I
was 1600 kilometres from medical help.

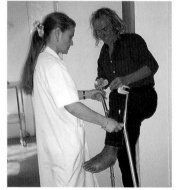

26

27

28

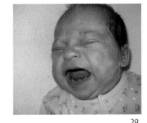

29

30

My family helps to keep me down to earth. Charlotte, Sebastian (above) and Clea (right) are woven around my heart like the tightly knit core of a climbing rope.

31

It was always my dream to climb, but wherever Sebastian's (above) and Clea's (right) hearts take them, I'll be there for them.

32

gave him a year on crutches. I lowered him down to the ground and, together with the mountain rescue team, we stretchered him out. There was blood all over the walls of the Tygerberg casualty room as we laid him down next to a pair of gangsters who had been at each other with knives. Ed's foot looked bad, all twisted at a funny angle. In the many bouts of surgery that followed, Ed steadfastly refused to have it fused because it would impede his climbing. It took a long time to heal and even now, when the weather changes, his ankle aches. It was a difficult and depressing time for him.

In 1983, Ed returned to university, this time to the University of Cape Town where his mother worked, and started a Bachelors degree in Archaeology. He would eventually earn a Masters in Archaeology in 1992, and a PhD in Botany in 1996, after 10 years working at the South African Museum. There was a brief wobble around 1998 when he considered quitting academia altogether to focus his energies on climbing, but in 2000 he joined UCT's department of Botany as a lecturer.

Ed met Nicky Allsop, a graduate student in Botany, in 1982, and the two of them fell for each other in a polite, shy and ham-handed way. Nicky is a tall, slight woman with an acerbic wit. She is also white, which meant back then that they couldn't do all the normal things that courting couples do, like go to movies, restaurants, pubs or the beach. So instead they went hiking and climbing together and I watched their relationship blossom in the hills and on the rocks where we spent our time climbing. Nicky completed a PhD in Botany and now works for the government's Agricultural Research Council, helping rural communities rehabilitate range-land.

In 1984 they moved to the Bo-Kaap, into an old, character-filled house called Rosedale, which had been built by his grandfather in 1894. Ed's father had been born there and the house had until recently belonged to Ed's aunt, the community midwife, 'Nurse February'. Surrounded by a colourful and vibrant Muslim community, who cared little about Ed and Nicky's contravention of the government's ban on mixed-race couples, they knew the names and family histories of nearly everyone on their street and they have been happily settled there ever since. Whenever I walk up the steps to their old teak front door under the shadow of Table Mountain, I steel myself before knocking. It's not easy to be around two intellectual PhD botanists and it takes a while to shake the feeling of being the dumbest person in the house. Luckily for me, they have two cats called Mali and Djenne, so named after our character-building trip to Mali in 1998, and together we keep each other company.

Ed and Nicky married in 1996. Ed called me in Seattle several weeks beforehand. "When are you coming over?" I told him the date I was due to arrive back in Cape Town and he set their wedding for the following day. They took their honeymoon in Nepal as part of the disastrous first South African Everest expedition, of which Ed and I both were members until fundamental disagreements with the leader, Ian Woodall, drove us to bow out before reaching the foot of the mountain. Ed still feels bitter about that experience, about how Woodall used the riptide of goodwill in the newly democratic South Africa for his own personal ends. I shrugged off the whole affair. It would have been great to have stood on top of Everest with Ed, but it wasn't meant to be. We went on other trips, to Mali, Cameroon, Kenya, Morocco, the USA and Europe, and I wouldn't trade them for anything.

Ed is the most optimistic South African I know. One bleak winter's morning in 1986, Ed and I pulled up to the border crossing between France and Italy. At the time apartheid South Africa was burning, it was in chaos. The army patrolled the townships and the government had virtually declared war on anything that threatened white power. The future looked bleak, or at least very violent in the short term. We handed over our South African passports to the Italian official, who examined our visas and then passed them back.

He looked Ed straight in the eye and asked in perfect English, "Are you going to go back to South Africa?"

"Yes"

"Why?"

Whenever Ed gets nervous, or upset, or when he feels something close to his heart, something in his body language changes. He starts to shake and twitch ever so slightly, as if someone has thrown a switch, sending a charge of electricity through him.

"I have to go back," he answered forthrightly, "It's my country."

He believes implicitly in South Africa and its future, dismissing harbingers of doom and gloom out of hand. Crime and political infighting are just the teething problems of a young democracy, he says. And he points to the massive developments in infrastructure in poor and rural areas made by the ANC in its first decade in power. His optimism is infectious and reassuring. At last Ed has a pivotal role as an educator in shaping a future that we both share, and I don't think it could be in better hands.

There are two Eds, the affable Ed I know from climbing and Ed the scientist, the doyen. This Ed is quite at home in a lab filled with large machines, strange equipment and computers. Here he runs multi-million-dollar research programmes. While graduate students and staff members bustle around, hard at work, it is Ed who is in charge. Technically, Ed is a plant eco-physiologist, but ultimately he and his team are trying to understand the potential effects that global climate change may have on our environment. Nowadays he travels to conferences all over the world on a schedule so busy that I have given up trying to keep track of where he is anymore. In between conferences, he lectures undergraduate students, tutors the honours classes, supervises the post-graduates, and still finds the time to secure research grants and do his own research. It's not surprising that Ed's head is full. He gets home exhausted every night, but he has simply replaced his climbing ambitions with academic ones. For the last 20 years he has thrown himself full tilt at academia and it's about to pay off. He will become a Professor of Botany in the near future. Through his own efforts and hard work, Ed has become an internationally respected scientist.

The impressive thing is, Ed is also an internationally respected climber and certainly the most famous black climber in the world. His picture has been on the cover of the British *Mountain Magazine*, a feature article appeared about him in the American *Outside* magazine, he's been on TV in the UK and the USA, and he is well known and well regarded overseas. Climbing luminaries always call on Ed when they come to South Africa. But he's divided on how he feels about this. While on one hand he enjoys the prestige, on the other he doesn't feel he's earned it. Ed feels that his global recognition as a climber hasn't been achieved on his climbing merit alone but rather on his circumstances as a black man in South African and it is something that keeps gnawing at him. Ed has always been ambitious, a fighter in his own quiet and steadfast way, in all that he does: growing up, climbing and his work, and it's become difficult not to approach the world like that. He's never satisfied and always pushing, but that's his nature and it's made him who he is. Maybe one day he'll be able to stop and see that all achievements are relative and that he's a good climber and he's earned all of our respect the hard way.

But Ed and I never talk about any of these real issues, these things close to our hearts, like the anger he felt at having been discriminated against. We just don't go there, preferring instead to let time smooth things over. I never knew the full depth of his lingering anger, a seething legacy of the apartheid years, until it all came to a head at the Mountain Club one evening in 2003. Tienie Versveldt, our friend and climbing partner of many years, stood up and said that the Mountain Club should apologise to Ed and the whole of the black community for its discriminatory actions during the apartheid years. Ed had been persuaded to join the MCSA in 1996, and after that he'd worked tirelessly to modernise the club and forge links between the older and younger generations. He became the pivotal point on which the future of South African climbing hinged, inspiring and mentoring a whole new generation of young climbers. And he enjoyed doing it. For all that he accomplished, the club awarded Ed the Gold Badge, their highest honour, and honorary life membership. But Ed's anger over the rebuttals by the club in his early years ran deep, although hidden. After Tienie opened the sluices, Ed's anger came flooding to the surface and he divorced himself from the MCSA shortly afterwards. The MCSA did issue a weak apology to him some months later, but Ed still hasn't been back to the organisation and he doesn't respond to any of their correspondence.

Ed's 50th birthday party in Montagu was quite an occasion. He stood up before his closest friends and his family and said that he was old and over the hill, and that although he still had ambitions, he knew that he wouldn't and couldn't realise them, so he was going to stop trying. What he meant was that he hadn't realised his full potential as a climber, but that he had accepted it and it was time to move on. Climbing has always been the central thread of Ed's life, the way he defined himself, and it was hard for him to let his ambitions go. What I should have told him at the time, but didn't, was that I felt the same way. We never get to properly finish the most important things in our lives, they just get taken away from us because we run out of time.

Ed and Nicky bought a house in Montagu in 2003. It's not far from the crags and they plan to retire there one day when they stop rushing about being at the top of their fields.

So what's Ed really like? He describes himself as "a tired and grumpy old man", but he's been saying that since I first met him. Ed has an understated way of presenting himself. He grumbles about "dragging his third class-body up some hill or other" whenever we go climbing, but look closer and behind his spectacles you'll see a childlike excitement. He lights up when he talks about climbing, or travelling through Africa, or his academic career. Look even closer and you'll see a passion that has driven him his whole life.

Back at my kitchen table it's well into the early hours. Ed pours another slug of whisky and says, "You know, youth, we've been through a lot together you and me, and you've turned out alright." I guess that will be the closest I'll get to a tacit approval of myself and what I've become after all these years. But it's enough.

Scattered around the house are sleeping children, plastic dinosaurs, dogs, puppies and the detritus of a normal, conventional life – a far cry from the weeks, months and years that we spent tied together into a rope, climbing high off the ground. Some of the routes we climbed are still indelibly printed on our memory, others have long since faded, but then Ed always said that he had a memory like a sieve. We've both mellowed like the whisky we're drinking, and I can see that Ed is slowly becoming comfortable with that. As Ed leaves he gives me a big hug and he shakes a little as he does so. It's Ed's way of saying thanks for being his friend.

Rust Never Sleeps

High in the Groot Drakenstein mountains of the Cape there is an ochre-coloured cliff called the Dragoon's Buttress, which overlooks the vineyards of the Franschhoek valley far below. Perched on the top of the mountain is an old tree, leaning, improbably, over the edge of the rock. A grizzled stone pine, it has survived ravaging wild fires over the years and I don't know how it's managed to grow so big, but it has, perhaps simply because it's a survivor in a harsh and precipitous place. It marks the end of the steepest part of the wall and it was around its gnarled trunk that I wrapped a sling when Ed and I free-climbed Rust Never Sleeps, becoming the first to climb this tricky and dangerous route under our own power on a scorching January day in 1983. The route had gone straight up the face, or nearly so, just as our friend Greg had envisioned and predicted. But what none of us could have envisioned back in those days when youth made us immortal was just how pivotal that brief period of time would be and how things were set to change in irreversible ways, for better and for worse. Rust Never Sleeps would become pivotal in my mind to loss.

Greg had an instinctive eye for a line, an innate knack of knowing exactly how to piece together the intricate jigsaw puzzle of rock features to climb new routes. The 1980s were the golden years of climbing in South Africa and Greg was king, climbing bold and visionary routes up the unclimbed walls of the Cape. It is traditionally said that climbing doesn't undergo rapid, revolutionary progress, but that progress is slow and steady, rather like a series of building blocks with each generation merely building on the progress of the last. But I disagree. In South Africa, under the shadow of apartheid and international isolation, climbing underwent a revolution unmatched by anything that had gone before. And Greg spearheaded it. He was a pioneering climber; somehow able to see lines in the negative spaces between existing routes where no one had gone before, and then to steadily climb them.

He was a 23-year-old computer operator for a start-up company called Infoplan. Tall and skinny, with a most unlikely, gangling build for a climber, his playful and easy-going nature concealed an extraordinary passion for climbing. Greg had a classic wit and an infectious grin and I liked him because even in the hairiest moments on the rock he would take a crack at the lighter side and make me laugh. His nickname was "Talks" and he really could talk. Greg discovered his incredible intuitive talent for climbing while still in high school at SACS (South African College Schools) in Cape Town, and later he would take the graveyard shift at work so that he could climb during the day. We were friends, but we were also rivals in an affable, light-hearted, and understated way, as Greg, Ed and I scrambled to fill in the blank spots on the map of Cape climbing. And even though we were buddies, it didn't stop us from each wanting to be first up unclimbed routes. One of the pressing blanks was the large unclimbed face on the Dragoon's Buttress.

So far it had proved elusive. The accomplished Cape climbers, Tony Dick and Roger Fuggle, first tried the line in the late 1970s, their attempt ending somewhere in the loose red bowl in the middle of the face. In the spring of 1982 Greg, Ed and I had a stab at it, but our attempt ended at a bulging pinched seam 40 metres from the top.

Then, unbeknownst to us, while Ed and I were making a valiant attempt on the upper wall at Milner Peak, Greg returned to the wall, with the solo legend Chris Lomax. Together they forced their way to the top, using gear pounded and wedged into the rock and hanging on it for aid, finishing the route at midnight. Ed and I were agreeably pissed off. Outraged that Greg had pinched our route while our backs were turned, we resolved that since most of their aided climbing had been done in the dark, we would go back and have a crack at free climbing it. We would climb the route in a better style, under our own power, using the ropes and equipment for protection only and not to aid us. It was our aim on the first attempt anyway. The stakes rose a notch. I imagined myself casually sauntering up to Greg at the Newlands Bridge. "Oh, by the way," I'd remark breezily, "We freed Rust Never Sleeps yesterday. It wasn't too bad actually, only grade 23. Why did you guys use so much aid?"

So a week later Ed and I started in the cool morning shadows and picked our way up the long slope that leads to the grass terraces that fall away from the base of the rock. While we were fighting our way through chest-high willow grass, Ed suddenly stopped and asked me what I thought of his idea to start studying at the University of Cape Town. He had enrolled for his degree in Archaeology and was in two minds about whether it was the right thing to do. At the time he was an industrial radiographer, trained to crawl inside metal pipes with an X-ray machine. I said he should go for it, consequences and funding be damned, because it would always work itself out later. Such was the advice from a 16-year-old. Years later, after I had completed my own degree and was considering a Masters in Philosophy at Oxford, Ed would give me the same advice, but I would choose to ignore it in order to climb instead. We reached the base of the rock and the excitement of attempting to free-climb it made me shiver. The sharp smell of uncoiled nylon ropes mixed with the taste of dry chalk dust as I started up. We climbed three easy pitches and then headed straight up into the tricky red heart of the buttress. As we climbed, the sun angled towards us, creeping up the wall faster than we could climb and the day turned hot. The rock was loose and the gear wasn't great, but it was all right because the climbing was not too difficult. Presently we found ourselves at our previous highpoint on a narrow ledge just below the steepest part of the cliff.

Above us was the nasty-looking pinched seam. It wasn't so much a crack as a fold in the rock and it would be like trying to climb the stitching on a pair of Levi's jeans. Ed looked worried as he fiddled in a poor belay: a peg hammered halfway in and a dubious number one stopper. "This thing won't hold a peanut butter sandwich," he muttered. On our previous attempt Greg had untied from the rope and sat down at the far end of the ledge with a sling tied round a small sapling. He told us with a grin that if one of us fell off, the belay would surely rip out and both Ed and I would plummet off the rock. But as he wasn't tied in he might get a bit thirsty where he was but at least someone would find him eventually. It was a dodgy place. I set off up the crack, aiding on gear that barely held my bodyweight until the seam ended abruptly. It was blank above. I found some anchors and lowered back down to find that Ed had been busily fortifying his anchors and had used almost all our gear to cobble together into his belay: "Might hold a peanut butter sandwich with jam on now." I pulled the ropes and tried to free-climb the pitch without hanging on any of the equipment. It's pretty psychological clipping your rope into gear that you know won't hold your weight in a fall, but I just kept going and held on for dear life. "Looking good kid," Ed yelled up with an unmistakable tremor to his voice. But it didn't feel good at all: it was steep and scary and I was pumped. I almost lost my nerve at the crux, but I hung on with every bit of strength I had and reached the top without falling. Ed followed up the pitch and I watched him fighting his way up the seam but he didn't fall off either and he arrived at my hanging belay with forearms pumped up like watermelons, veins like a roadmap, and with a manic glint of triumph behind his specs.

By now it was desperately hot: the January sun beat mercilessly down on us out of a blister-white summer sky, scorching our necks, parching our throats and swelling our feet in our climbing shoes. The cliff faced exactly northwest and there wasn't a cloud to shield us from the relentless afternoon sun that pierced our eyelids. I blinked away the black spots, wiped the sweat out of my eyes and hung uncomfortably in my harness while Ed climbed his way left along the rail. Greg had left some pegs behind during their night-time ascent, and Ed clipped his rope into them as fixed protection. Following him I lurched from hold to hold: they were thin and you couldn't get your fingers into the crack until right at the end. I fought a rising pump in my tired forearms but was determined not to fall off. I followed the rail, and the route was free.

I led the last easy pitch up to the old pine tree, and then we scrambled to the top where we huddled in the shade of a boulder next to the trig beacon. It really was hot. We had climbed the route free, and so technically our climb had been done in a better and purer style than Greg's first ascent, but up there on the baking summit it really didn't seem to matter anymore. It felt like we were splitting hairs and the style of ascent seemed unimportant now that we had all climbed the route. Ed somehow managed to open a can of tuna with a knife blade peg and we sucked down the oily water and chunks of fish. It was such a simple moment: there we were, two friends, with the unstated presence of Greg hovering around us, at the top of a difficult and dangerous route up a large rock wall sharing a can of tuna. It marked the end of an age of innocence in a way, and now with hindsight, I will always see past and future blending together with a sharp poignancy on that hot, sweat-soaked afternoon.

We were so young then. Sitting under that boulder the world held so much promise and there were so many choices. The future shone so bright, and none of us knew how it would turn out. But the two of us, young men on the cusp of the future, thought of none of this. How could we have, as we walked down the steep slope through the pooling heat above the fynbos, down to the car and dusty dirt roads that churned thirsty air as we drove into the night to the nearest café and drank two litres of Coke apiece without stopping for air.

The following month Ed would change the course of his life completely when he enrolled at UCT to study Archaeology, launching his academic career. I look forward to the day, in the not too distant future, when he will finally become a professor because I have always been proud of that bold career move he made.

The following month, too, Greg's girlfriend, Beverly Opperman, would be killed on Table Mountain at the age of 22, after slipping while climbing up Arrow Final, an easy route beneath the cable-way. Greg was belaying her and he was the first to reach her as she hung on the rope with grievous head injuries. I don't know what he must have felt at the time, but he went to pieces afterwards. Greg's mother phoned to tell me what had happened and I went to him immediately, sitting in his room and awkwardly trying to comfort his skinny, lanky frame, which was wracked with sobbing tears. I didn't know what to do or say, so I just held his hand.

Greg never talked about the accident to me. A few months later we were opening a new route called 'Oceans of Fear' and while I was taking a really long time leading a pitch, Greg quietly chipped her name into the red sandstone high off the ground with a hammer. It's still there: a discreet sentinel to Greg's silent grief. Bev was a beautiful young woman with the world at her feet and in my mind she will always be frozen at 22 years old, laughing in dappled sunlight filtering through old oak trees in the Cederberg, where we went the weekend before she was killed.

Six months after Bev's accident, exactly to the day, Greg himself was killed. Ed broke the news to me, pulling up on a Sunday morning on his motorcycle outside my mother's house in Claremont to tell me that my friend was dead. He said that Greg had been descending the south side of Le Droites in the French Alps in the late afternoon, when treacherous, slushy snow gave way under him, sending him sliding and bouncing down the slope, unable to stop himself. He fell 150 metres, and in doing so broke his neck. It seemed unreal to me, almost unbelievable, and after Ed drove away I sat in the garden for a long time tracing the veins on a leaf and thinking about him. That day the mid-winter August sun had a subdued brightness to it that didn't seem right. I went inside and reread a letter he had sent me a few days before in his tiny, spidery handwriting. And then I headed up Table Mountain, alone, to wander aimlessly for hours and hours, my chest aching with a depressing sense of loss, until I was too tired to feel anything more.

At the time the fragility of all our lives didn't sink in fully because, with the blinkers of youth clamped firmly over my eyes, I still saw myself and everyone around me as immortal. It was as if Greg and Bev had been with us at the edge of an ocean, revelling in the pounding waves, and then suddenly, when the next wave washed out, they were gone. I often wonder where those two would be if they were still alive today. Would they still be together? And what would they be doing with their lives? I miss them both. I liked them and I know that we would be friends even now. Not long ago I ran into Greg's mother, Nora Lacey, a rail-thin, feisty 65-year-old retiree. She misses him too. We were the ones left behind, to grieve in our own ways. I can't begin to imagine what it must be like to lose a child and I hope it never happens to me.

Some years ago I had a cup of tea with Professor Marthinus Versfeld, professor emeritus of philosophy at the University of Cape Town and my long-time friend and climbing partner Tienie's father. He had taught one of my philosophy classes on the principles of logic at the university. He was a wise man with a sharp and playful wit. We talked about youth and age. His rheumy eyes and white-shocked hair belied the passion he still felt for the mountains. He talked about walking up Table Mountain every day until one day he couldn't anymore. "Time catches up with you so quickly," he said. So we resolve to live each moment to its fullest, but what happens when you try that, and even then, you are still somehow left half-filled as time erodes our youth and casts a yellow patina around the edges of our memories. We can never go back. Perhaps, in a way, it is kinder to die young with our dreams and potential permanently suspended, than to remain forever unsettled by our transience.

Three years after Greg's death, I was descending from the Droites at the start of my alpine career when an eerie sense told me that I was standing near the spot where Greg's life had come to an end. It was also late afternoon as we scrambled down over some rocks below a snowfield. And I just knew. A seventh sense; the one that keeps watch over us in the mountains and connects all of us in wild places, let me know that it had all happened there. The slope looked so peaceful and benign. The sun glinted off the broad expanse of soft snow and the mountains were huge all around. It was a beautiful place without any tangible hint of the young life that had been lost there. I felt sad, but mostly tired and hungry and we continued on, and the loss only hit me later. When I got down I went to the cemetery in

Chamonix, passing all the luminary headstones to the grave of my young friend and I sat with my memory of him and wondered why it had worked out that way.

Not long ago, some 20 years after we first climbed Rust Never Sleeps, I stood on a small ledge just big enough for my feet and peered straight down over the edge to where our route wound its way through the ochre-coloured rock in the dizzy plunge beneath me. I hadn't been back since that hot January day all those years ago. In fact, I hadn't given it a thought in my relentless quest to climb. Twenty years is a long time, more than half my life, and so much has happened and so much has changed since those early climbing days. I have spent most of my life climbing all over the world. I have made friends in high places and lost many, people who simply didn't return from the mountains. Now, coming back to the top of Rust Never Sleeps and seeing the wizened old pine tree sparked a wildfire of memories long buried. I thought of our fleeting youth and unlimited dreams and of Greg, Ed and myself as young men holding the future in our hands as we clutched tightly onto the red rock that dropped away beneath us. Time had moved on, so relentlessly, and so quietly, that I felt almost as if I were looking into the lives of strangers.

I threw a rock off the edge and watched intently for the puff of rock dust on impact. "Nine point five seconds", read the stopwatch, 300 metres to the ground. I wasn't there to climb. I had come to BASE-jump off the cliff in a wingsuit: a space-age flying suit that catches the air and turns the jumper's body into a 'wing', slowing down the freefall and propelling you away from the cliff face. I zipped up my suit and strapped on my parachute. How could I have known back then that two decades later I would stand on the edge about to jump off? Our lives are filled with unexpected twists as they meander over the years. I held out my wings like the statue of Christ in Rio and gazed at the Helderberg and at Franschhoek so far below. Why had I not noticed how postcard pretty it was when we were here before? I looked at the horizon, breathed out, and gently jumped off the edge into nothing but air.

After a few seconds I started to move away from the cliff as the air pressure turned my body into a wing. I was flying now. I soared down towards the fynbos, easily clearing the grassy terraces at the base of the cliff, and I was filled with an amazing sense of peace. My wings were stable; I was relaxed and flying close to the ground, but perfectly in control. I flew down the long slope that we had walked up all those years ago. As it started to flatten out, I saw that I wouldn't gain any more altitude and I reached behind me to open my parachute. After a short canopy flight, I landed with an abrupt stop safely in the fynbos, and then I turned to look back up at the cliff. The first thing that caught my eye was the old pine tree hanging over the edge of the rock.

My flight somehow opened a sluice between the 16-year-old boy I was and the man I am now. As the waters rushed in, heartache and loss swirled with a bittersweet happiness, sorrow and regret mixing with joy. Everything felt so different looking back through the clarity of two decades. I mourned the loss of innocence, and youth, and friends, while rejoicing in the pure happiness that being young and time spent with my friends had so briefly brought me. I saw all the choices I had made, incrementally narrowing the course of my life until I became a different person. I couldn't and wouldn't ever go back again. Then, as I turned away and began to walk down the last of the fynbos slope, the waters started to recede until there was nothing left except a yawning gulf of memory between now and then.

Rust never sleeps: it relentlessly corrodes the things we have made, things we thought would last a long time. It's an inevitable process of decay. The pegs we left on the route will become the rusty markers of a human passage many years ago and our jumps off the cliff are as traceless and transient as the flight path of birds. Time is also like rust: it never sleeps either.

Now when I watch my small son and the joy he gives me as he takes his first unsteady steps, I know Rust Never Sleeps belongs to another lifetime. And I'm happy with that.

Cloudwalkers

It was a beautiful autumn morning on the top of Table Mountain. Bright sunshine washed over us, making us squint into the glaring light as we stood on the Lookout, a flat, jutting promontory right on the edge of a sheer 150-metre cliff face overlooking the buildings of Cape Town and Table Bay far below. The Lookout is one of the exit points for BASE jumping off Table Mountain. A few hundred metres from the cable-car station, it's a perfect place from which to run, with as much power as you can muster, and then leap into space with a parachute strapped to your back and your heart in your mouth.

The day was windless and still, excellent conditions for jumping, except for a menacing layer of fog that was rapidly rolling in over the city and up the lower slopes of the mountain, threatening to scupper our plans. I was with my BASE-jumping friend, Karl, and we both watched the cloud bank swirl and thicken as it curled around Lion's Head and Devil's Peak. It was almost surreal standing high above the ocean of cloud that now bridged the Indian and Atlantic oceans by way of the Cape Flats. The cloudbank quickly obscured our landing area, the thin ribbon of Tafelberg Road 600 metres below. All our visual references had now become buried under a thick, broiling mass of cloud. All we could see was white.

BASE jumps are always tense. The objects you are jumping from are low, which means timing is tight – you have one parachute and one chance to get it right. It comes with significantly more risk than similar sports like skydiving or paragliding because the margins are so much tighter and because you are in close proximity to your launch platform, whether it's a mountain, a building or an antenna. The whole idea is to have all of the variables carefully calculated and plotted before you leap off the edge into air. You need to know exactly what you are going to do from exit right through to landing. Reaction times are short, and there is very little time for changes of plan. The moment you step away from this narrow predictability, the likelihood of injury rises sharply.

We knew this well and, despite not being able to see the landing area, we strapped on our parachutes, did a final gear check and then settled down to wait. Occasionally we caught a glimpse of the road when wisps of cloud wafted apart to reveal the tall pine trees alongside the snaking asphalt, before shutting down into a rolling blanket of white again. We waited and waited and waited, peering intently into that ever changing glacier of white air, hoping for a large enough hole to open in the clouds to allow us three minutes of clarity to fly down.

My cut-off time was 9am. After that I decided I would pack up my gear and run down the mountain. At one minute to nine a hole appeared and I saw the road. I looked at Karl, nodded, and then without hesitating I ran off the edge into space...

No matter how many jumps you do, that first second of freefall is unique. You are momentarily weightless, impossibly suspended in still air. And then, just like cartoon characters, you drop.

I fell for three seconds. "One Thousand. Two Thousand. Three Thousand." It's not a very long time, but those three seconds dragged out forever as I plunged towards the earth. Each second felt like an hour until the self-preservation voice inside my head kicked in: "Time's Up! Pull Now! Quickly! Now! Now! Now!" and all the alarm bells went off at once.

I reached behind me and threw my pilot chute quickly and violently into the air. After that there was nothing else I could do except plummet and wait for the parachute to open. It felt like I was falling through a trapdoor at the mercy of the hangman, the red-hot knowledge of danger like a noose around my neck. Time slowed right down and everything happened in silent slow motion. I looked at the ground, which was becoming blurry with speed, and I heard, with absolute clarity, the sound of my parachute opening above me, sucking, and filling with air, until it opened with a '*Thwack!*'.

It was a perfect opening. I was facing away from the cliff and I flew away, relief washing over me. I was still alive. Karl had jumped just after me and I saw his canopy flying off to the right. Even though it's every man for himself in the sky, it was comforting to see him flying up there with me.

And now we were cloudwalkers, slicing through the clear calm air high above a magic carpet of clouds that stretched out to the horizon. It was a soft white blanket, gently luring and tempting us to land on it and get whisked away to some fabled Arabian paradise. But I quickly snapped out of my euphoria when I looked at the cloud below. During the jump the hole above our landing area had disappeared and we found ourselves suspended, horrifyingly, above a world of white. I felt a surge of fear wash through my body.

My mind began racing: computing and calculating distances, angles and trajectories of where to land as I slowly sank towards that soft white deadly pillow that obscured any view of a safe landing area. Down to the left I could just make out the ghostly grey shape of the lower cableway station in the mist and I turned towards it because it gave me an aim, a visual reference to the road instead of simply flying blind. Near the cableway station though, the road twists and winds, flanked by tall trees on the uphill side and at that time of the morning parked cars would be lining both sides of the road. By now I'd abandoned the open landing area where we usually touched down more than a kilometre along the road to the right in favour of what I could see.

Panic was bubbling below the surface as I slipped down into the cloud. Parachutes fly very fast, and you can get badly injured in a blind collision. I had no idea how far above the road I was, and a little voice in the back of my head kept repeating: "I don't want to get hurt; I don't want to get hurt." I could feel the moisture on my face and hands as my vision dropped to zero. Everything turned white and I tasted water in the air. It was chilling, but there was no time for anything but pure concentration.

Thinking fast, with grim focus, I lined myself up blindly to where I thought the road should be and for long seconds that felt like forever, I flew completely blind, staring desperately into the unforgiving white fog. With my heart in my mouth I tensed for a collision, waiting, waiting for something to see. And then suddenly in a murky instant, I caught a blur of gloomy green just below me. In a flash I knew where I was, on the uphill side of the trees, and then I saw the subdued grey of the curving road below. Instantly I turned the canopy 180 degrees, feet skimming over the treetops, and carved a further 90 degrees to follow the curve of the road. There was hardly any time to flare and I pounded into the road, hard and fast, but on my feet.

The parachute deflated. Relief that I was safe flooded over me. Mist swirled in shredded wisps around me in that damp foggy netherworld under the cloud, while a veiled obscure sun tried valiantly to burn it away from high above. With shaking hands and racing nerves, I packed my rig into the stash-bag and walked along the road to see where Karl had landed. I was a little worried about him, but Karl is very calm and experienced. It turned out he'd had just enough visibility, together with a good measure of instinct, to put himself down on the long straight road near our usual landing area.

We were both safe. We had broken one of the cardinal rules of BASE jumping, but had emerged unscathed. You could put some of that down to skill and experience, but a lot simply came down to pure luck. We walked back to our cars and our day-to-day lives along the still damp road. We were firmly back on earth, but inside our spirits were cloudwalking.

We moderns, we half-barbarians;
We are in the midst of our bliss
Only when we are most in danger.

FRIEDRICH NIETZSCHE, 1844–1900
BEYOND GOOD AND EVIL

Julie

Two small figures are delicately balanced on a small ice-ledge, bent over packing their bivouac gear after their fourth night roped onto a big ice wall. They are 26 rope lengths up, more than a thousand dizzying metres above the glacier, on the North Buttress of Mount Hunter, a cold, unforgiving mountain that rises out of a vast wilderness in central Alaska. And they are still a very long way from the top. The two are indistinguishable from each other, bundled as they are in bulky winter clothing with cumbersome packs on their backs, but they are a man and a woman. The dawn is grey and the sky filled with swirling snow. One of the figures starts climbing, the sound of his ice pick ringing in the muffled silence and soon he is swallowed by the mist as he climbs into The Vision, a complex series of steep and discontinuous ice runnels. The ice is green, frosted with new snow, and it shatters into white shards as his dull tool impacts the cold surface.

I first met Julie Brugger in Chamonix in France. She had come to the Alps hoping to find climbing partners in the muddy campgrounds where we all lived in leaking tents and appalling squalor for months on end because we had dreams of climbing the lofty alpine spires that towered above us. She came up to me as I sat under a tree and asked whether I was looking for a climbing partner. She was pretty, with long dark hair, but she talked loudly and there was a hard edge to her. My first thought was "Oh no, another loud American, and a woman at that," but I was intrigued by her, and so I said yes. In a way I was looking for a climbing partner, because I'd gone there alone and had been climbing with various partners or solo for several months. We did a short alpine rock climb the following day and I was impressed by her strength and enthusiasm. After that we climbed bigger and harder routes in Chamonix and in Switzerland. She was keen for anything and everything.

Somewhere between climbing Mont Blanc and the Matterhorn we became lovers, as I fell in love with her intense passion for life and her funny, almost goofy, manner. When she laughed her whole face cracked up and the laughter came from her soul. She made salad sandwiches so huge that you had to warm up your jaw before tackling them. As we got to know each other, we talked all the time, about anything and everything, so much so that people in the mountain bivouac huts asked us to shut up. My alpine ambitions dovetailed with hers and we did an incredible amount of climbing that summer, climbing dozens of alpine walls and then spending three months rock climbing in southern France when the weather turned bad in the mountains. In Julie I recognised a similar soul to my own; someone who felt isolated and different to other people as I did and who cherished her freedom. Like me, she preferred to follow her heart rather than convention.

At the end of the season we parted in London, and I knew inside that it wasn't a permanent goodbye. She went back to America and I to South Africa. But I felt confused and restless at home; my world had expanded and I wanted to be out there exploring it. We wrote letters describing our separate lives and I dreamed of the big wide world beyond, and all the climbing that I could do with my new friend. The connection remained strong and I couldn't get her out of my mind. Even climbing couldn't distract me. We arranged to meet in Peru the following summer.

The hooded, bundled figure in The Vision places a mechanical camming device for protection. As he climbs further up, it falls out, its mechanism frozen immobile, leaving him at risk of a lengthy fall. He shuts it out of his mind and finishes the pitch, tying himself into ice screws safely twisted into the ice and yelling into the snowy void for her to start climbing. An hour passes and then the second figure emerges out of the snow and wind, melting the icy mantle around the rope with her mouth so that the jumar clamps that she is using to climb up the rope can grip. Silent and cold, they exchange gear in a well-versed routine that needs no words and he climbs a narrow smear of ice, which grows ever steeper. Just at the vertical fulcrum it runs into impassable overhanging rock. Twenty metres to the left he can see another ice runnel breaking through the rock band. He places a knife blade peg into a thin crack, clips the rope into it, and lowers himself a few metres back down again. And then he starts to swing back and forth on the rope, building speed. His crampons screech on the rock as he runs across the wall in the growing arc of the pendulum. On the final swing he launches himself violently in the direction of the runnel, reaching out for it with his axe. Thud! His tool impacts the ice and the rope tugs at his harness. Snowy waves of spindrift avalanche over him as he heaves himself up into the groove.

Julie is intense, the most intense person I have ever known. She is a small, muscle-packed woman who works out every day and has almost limitless enthusiasm and energy for whatever project she focuses on. She never gives up. Julie succumbed to the lure of the mountains while she was studying computer science at the University of Washington, and high, wild places have become her first and only real home. Shy and reserved, she has always been uncomfortable around people and she's often seen as a loner, but that's just what people see on the surface. To her few friends she is beautiful, loyal, committed and irrepressibly funny. She is also deeply intellectual and intuitive: someone who senses everything from the heart, it's her antenna and she uses it to navigate the world.

On the morning of the fourth day the two figures reach The Shaft, the crux of the North Buttress, a narrow 150-metre-high chimney. It's as high as a 40-storey building, ice slicing through an overhanging rock buttress for three vertical and overhanging pitches. It's beyond challenging. Hanging by his arms on ice pick tips wedged just a few millimetres into the ice, with the barest purchase from the points of the crampon spikes clipped to his boots, he climbs rhythmically upwards, arms tiring from the effort. One arm swings. *Whack!* The ice pick goes in. He raises a foot. *Smack!* The crampon digs into the ice. He passes an overhanging bulge of ice from which a glittering chandelier of ice needles dangle. The climbing is exhilarating and wild. Their world, their real world, consists only of a steep ribbon of white ice cleaving two dark granite buttresses, and nothing else matters or exists other than the immediacy of the present.

Determined to join her in Peru, I borrowed money to book my plane ticket and paid it back by working in the old slate quarry on Table Mountain. A group of us climbers earned "danger pay" by hanging off ropes while we precariously chiselled away lethal slabs of rock to be used as flagstones in Cape Town's historic castle. We reunited in Lima airport. It was strange to see her again. She felt softer and her hair was longer than the image I'd held in my mind for so long. We travelled to the small town of Huaraz high in the Cordillera Blanca, the knobbly, snow-capped spine of the Andes, where we revelled in each other's company, climbing high peaks and flying our paragliders from the summits. It was an intoxicating freedom. Julie had once said her philosophy of life was "to get a good tan and to have one of each", whatever it may be. It wasn't too far from the truth in Peru, where we lived outdoors under a limitless sky and tried one of everything. I was happier than I had ever been before.

The two figures are high on the North Buttress now. Two planes of a 2000-metre wall have come together to form a prow laced with ice and veined with narrow ice runnels that barely connect in their elegant sweep up to the summit. It is an alpine climber's dream, a steep technical climb up what is probably the finest ice wall in the western hemisphere. Despite many attempts, the North Buttress had only been climbed twice before and it had earned a reputation of being a formidable Alaskan test piece.

After three months of intense climbing in Peru, we flew off Huascaran Norte with our paragliders. And Julie broke her arm on landing.

A week later we were married. It just seemed to happen, although it took several days of wading through arcane Peruvian bureaucracy to get there. To us there was so little logic to the red tape that our bid to be married became tinted with that intangible Latin sense of magic, the sparkling strangeness that pervades the novels of Isabel Allende and Gabriel Garcia Márquez. There were obstacles left and right and we eventually landed up at the police chief. Flat out impossible, he said. Then he looked at Julie's arm and asked me in Spanish whether I had hit her. No. He rubbed his ample belly and asked if she were pregnant. No. So why do you two gringos want to get married? We love each other. A twinkle appeared in his eye and he started to smile. "Come to think of it, there might be a way in which we can bend the rules. *Si*, I think this could be a good idea!" Rubber stamps thudded into stacks of paper as thick as my arm and doors opened as if by magic.

Julie and I were married by the mayor in his grubby office in Huaraz. I was 21 and she was 37. I said "Si" and so did she and suddenly we were married. We were wearing our climbing clothes and Julie's arm was in a cast, but our smiles were wide because we were happy and young and our heads were filled with dreams. Afterwards we went out for dinner with two New Zealander climbing friends who had been the *dos testigos* (two witnesses) at the wedding. We had *Pollo a'la Brassa* (roast chicken) in a typical grimy Peruvian restaurant.

After that we climbed all over the world. It was the best years of our lives, and in a way Julie was the finest and most complete climbing partner I have ever had because of the spiritual affinity that we shared. But, like the fleeting passing of youth, I didn't realise the full significance of what we had until afterwards, when it was too late. The mountains became our "real" world, a world of new and uncertain places and doing what we loved. The everyday routine of normal life had become the "other world" from which we would flee as often as we could. We were modern day adventurers, only finding our bliss in the wide-open, in harsh, uncomfortable places where our spirits could soar without constraint.

It is three in the morning and the two exhausted figures are pitching their tiny tent on a narrow strip of ice. They are grateful to be able to sleep in a tent after the four previous nights spent awkwardly in the open, pinned to the ice wall. They are also grateful to be over the tricky climbing on The Vision, where the ice had been so milky-hard that ten blows with the axe barely chinked its immutable frozen face. It is snowing incessantly. In the night, spindrift avalanches come whooshing out of the whiteness and slam into the tent, making sleep intermittent and stressful. Every half hour one of them has to leave the warmth of their sleeping bag to dig the accumulated spindrift out from behind the tent to prevent them being forced over the abyss. And so they catnap restlessly, as rime ice slowly grows into hanging white feathers on the inside of the tent.

When Julie was excited she would talk, a stream of unedited thoughts would become a torrent of words as she said anything that came to mind. I loved to watch her in a good mood, such a change from her otherwise shy and reserved nature, and she was always in a good mood in the mountains. The mountains and wild, open places were her elixir, her magic fountain from which she drew her youth. At 40, Julie looked half her age because she never felt old. She will always be young, peering brightly into the future, dreaming up the next adventure and sharing it with her chosen partner, friend and companion. I was that person for a long time until our futures untied themselves and toppled off the edge.

After two days pinned down by the storm in their tent they realise they have to move before a really big avalanche sweeps them away. The frozen tent takes up most of the haulbag, but there is space because almost all the food is gone. They climb up into the storm, unable to see, unable to hear, each in their own hooded world, for six diagonal pitches. They stay close to the vertical rock wall above them, as huge spindrift avalanches sail out over their heads and explode with a crumpling sound against the ice field below. It is like surfing through an icy supertube 1800 metres off the ground Their Gore-Tex clothing has frozen into suits of armour. Late the next day the two ice-encrusted and exhausted figures emerge onto the northeast ridge after seven horrible pitches up the avalanche grooves on the final ice fields. On the ridge the storm seems to be abating. It has stopped snowing and they catch glimpses of Denali through the swirling clouds. They dig a big flat platform for the tent in the snow and share their final meal, a Snickers bar, in silence.

When Julie was happy she would sing. She sang the "Ballad of the Sandman" the way Joan Baez used to sing it, her strong, clear voice ringing out about love and loss, the haunting words echoing off the icy blue mountains all around us and resonating into the isolation we had imposed upon ourselves. We had moved beyond the reach of humanity and any human security as the two of us huddled in our tent on the North Buttress, because that was us, Julie and I, at our best, in a vast and empty universe in the middle of Alaska. We couldn't know what tomorrow would bring, we were out of food and nearly out of fuel, but we would continue. And still Julie sang. I don't know how she remembered all the verses but she did and I felt reassured by her voice and her presence. I saw the edge of vast darkness that night, a darkness that lay beyond the twilight and the ice outside and I didn't see any God in that black void. I sensed the essence of what our existence really is and it was frightening. I was glad Julie was there.

They awake to weak sunlight and a strong wind for their summit day. Boiling clouds over Foraker indicate that the storm is not over, but it holds off as they break a trail in the snow for 10 hours up the ridge to the summit plateau. It is desolate beyond belief. Four hours more and they stand on the summit of Mount Hunter, the consummation of nine days of brutal effort. There is a surreal detachment as they stand there: 2800 metres and 27 kilometres of perilous ground lie between them and the food in their base camp. Sad and tired, they turn away from fantasies of a quick flight down by paraglider and begin to descend the other side of the summit pyramid.

Three days later, the two still haven't left the summit plateau. In the whirling white world of the storm they haven't been able to find the narrow couloir that leads onto the West Ridge and the way home. They haven't eaten for four days. Thin, fine snow hurtles through the air, whipped into an icy vortex by the wind. Their steps are erratic. A black hole marks the crevasse into which one of them fell. There is a complete visual shutdown and no way to tell where the sky ends and earth begins, no landmarks to show the way. There are just the two dark muffled figures at each end of the rope. The leading figure plops down into the snow, overcome by a futile tiredness. Will they ever get off this damned mountain? They pitch the tent and lie down weak with hunger for their thirteenth interminable day and night. They are bivouacked right on the knife-edge crest of the ridge. That night he dreams of being blown off the edge. It's as if the world itself is a flat, frozen wasteland with the two of them camped at the very end of it, the only people left alive, struggling, struggling until eventually a huge storm hits them and then they have no chance at all.

Julie and I were a team. We weren't a tremendously efficient team, but we were partners in a special way because we knew each other so well and we depended on each other in subtle ways. Days earlier I had been ploughing a trench through bottomless wind slab snow, wading step after laboured step in the approach to the start of the North Buttress. It was exhausting, soulless drudgery and I had been on the verge of giving up, when Julie said quietly from behind "We're getting there", as if she could read my thoughts. Julie would never give up on anything, but her tenacity has always been tempered by a strong and rational appraisement and she would never allow her determination to drive her into danger. Her calm, moderating and very experienced influence almost certainly kept me alive during the years we were together. Without her I may have driven myself over the edge in the hot pursuit of pure ambition. Alpinism is not only about physical hardship, deprivation and suffering, it's also about the connections that are so strongly forged with our partners up there. Our partnership was a once in a lifetime union. We shared another world together, our real world, and just by looking at her I knew that she felt the same way.

Up on the summit plateau he awakes with a start. There is no more wind! Hot breath melts the tent's frozen zipper and a head pops out. The Alaskan midnight sky is an icy cobalt blue and refracted light makes the ridge below glimmer like white fire. It is totally clear! Gloom and despair at being trapped in a white prison evaporate instantly. They pack in manic haste and continue descending, but euphoria quickly dissipates into exhaustion. As the sun rises to a perfect day, they mechanically perform the motions of descent. For 28 hours they wade, wallow, and down-climb through soft snow, belly-crawl across crevasses and fight off exhaustion for long, endless kilometres. Their camp is at the top of a final heartbreaker hill. They labour their way up that long slope, resting often in the bleached blue twilight of the night while the world sleeps, and with each exhausted step more of the North Buttress slips into view above them.

It is 3am when they unzip their base-camp tent 14 days after leaving it. The first cup of sweet tea hits their senses with an orgasmic jolt as the sugar rushes into their blood. They brew into the morning, cup after cup, revitalising themselves after five foodless days. For days afterwards a curious depression settles over them. Unable to recall the feeling of exhilaration during the first few days of climbing, it is almost as if the route, and even more so the hellish descent, had sucked away their souls, leaving a numbness behind.

It was only months later, when the memory of being utterly wasted had faded, that we could finally see what it really was: one of the best ice climbs of our lives.

Julie and I were married for nine years and it's difficult to pinpoint when it all started to unravel. Partly we were too compatible, too much alike, and partly I always held some part of myself back. Subtle shifts occurred in our relationship until we became more like siblings than lovers, and I began to feel constricted. I strained to express myself as someone different from her. She saw the cracks appearing and reacted with an innate fear of abandonment, and the inevitable downward spiral began. The glue that had held us together was climbing, but eventually even that bond began to weaken. I could never really understand why. We tried and tried, but eventually I gave up and walked away because it felt like I was being buried alive by an avalanche. I had married too young, and ironically, while I could commit without hesitation to the uncertainty and danger of being on an alpine wall, I couldn't commit to loving Julie. I broke her heart and that will always be my life's regret.

Julie remains one of my closest friends. Long after we had climbed Mount Hunter and parted ways I received a letter in her familiar handwriting. On the pages were salt traces of dried tears. She wrote about her layers of sadness and how they could be unexpectedly pierced by something like a picture of Mount Hunter, to unleash waves of unutterable loss.

Neither of us will ever get over it completely.

I have an image of Julie that says more than words ever can: Just under the summit of Mount Hunter, after we'd dropped our packs on a small col, I turned to kick steps into the last few metres to the top and happened to glance at her. She was gazing out over the vast, white expanse of Alaskan mountains. And underneath all the bulky extreme-weather clothes, the gear, the sunglasses and the inevitable fatigue, I saw a childlike, impish grin. She was in bliss. There was nowhere else she would rather be. And I wouldn't have wanted to be there with anyone else.

The Rule Book

It was in Yosemite one calm autumn morning that I met Buddy and Dorothy Eisner. They stepped out of their Winnebago mobile home in the campsite next to ours and introduced themselves in that cheerful way that Americans do. Recently retired, they had taken the long road west to California in search of a lifetime's worth of postponed adventure. Buddy had been a hydraulic pump engineer and Dot a homemaker in the flat corn lands of Des Moines, Iowa. Buddy had served in World War II as a sapper in Europe, rebuilding bridges and clearing bombed-out buildings during the Allied advance on Berlin. On his return he married Dot, his high school sweetheart, and in their 43 years of marriage they had had four children. All of them were grown up and had moved away. Of their three sons, two were in the computer software business, the other was a lawyer, and their daughter was a nurse. Their eyes lit up as they told me about their children and their three grandchildren.

Theirs had probably been a long and happy life and they seemed like good people who had given their best to everything they did. I looked at Buddy and saw a frail but sprightly old man, plaid work shirt stretched tightly across his pot belly and rheumy eyes pale blue under a CAT baseball cap. His hip had been replaced the previous year.

Nonetheless, I felt a tweak of sadness for this pair who had played by convention, doing everything right and working their whole adult lives for this, an all-too-brief period of freedom in the twilight of their lives. They had come to Yosemite to feel the wonder of that giant valley carved out of granite, to see the lofty pines and smell the wood smoke of a thousand campfires. Buddy pottered around organising his camp site for a while, got the makings of his fire ready, and then went inside to watch some television, in a routine probably not much different to that at home.

Julie drank some more tea, I had another cup of coffee, we organised the rack, and then went climbing on The Cookie. It seemed such a strange contradiction to see these two old people on their quest for adventure, unwittingly finding themselves solidly in the middle of society's unwritten book of rules. They had spent their younger years providing security for themselves and their children, only to finally find a measure of freedom in their retirement, after they had grown old. And while I could understand it perfectly, I just couldn't relate to doing it that way.

It is true that climbing tends to be a magnet for a certain type of personality. It attracts those who are slightly anarchic, somewhat disdainful of the rest of society and able to get by on very little as they exist on the margins of the book of rules. I've run into them frequently in some very odd places, the kind of people who don't really fit in. But the common thread among us all is that we took our retirement first, while we were young and spry, mortgaging our futures and planning to work it off sometime, a live-now-pay-later attitude. Some never get to come out of retirement, they die young in the mountains, or become bums and derelicts. Most, though, move back onto the pages of the rule book as they get older.

I retired at 21 after finishing my studies. Even now, I wonder how I survived, but I wouldn't trade it for anything, living on the margins of society, eating on pavements, sleeping in tents, portaledges, or cramped bivouacs high off the ground. Working as a cabinetmaker just long enough to pay for the next ticket, my dreams lining themselves up like tin soldiers on a shelf. I've been to some of the wildest places on earth, mostly paid for by the sweat of my own labours, but sometimes with adventure grants, and occasionally as part of fully funded expeditions. But somehow I always managed to get myself into those places where money has no value; into the mountains and the air. And the time spent there has been priceless. They say that youth is wasted on the young, but I disagree. For those who have taken their time and maximised it while they were still young, strong, free, and very much alive, retirement can't last long enough. It all becomes relative, a toss up between freedom and security. My answer would be to get out and live while you can and worry about the consequences later, because there will never be another chance.

It was only years later, when I was well into my early retirement, that I finally found a perspective on this relativity between freedom and security. And I needed my freedom and my youth to physically get to where I learned this lesson, to where I got a view from the outside. I had been climbing in the Eastern Karakoram Himalaya in Pakistan for three months when our expedition descended out of the mountains to reach the small Balti village of Hushe. At 3000 metres it lies isolated at the end of the only road into that part of the mountains. Set on a steep hillside among verdant terraces of apricots, the village had mud-walled buildings and labyrinthine alleys. It probably didn't look very different from how it had looked in the fourteenth century during the reign of Tamerlane, the Mongol conqueror of Central Asia who'd swept through the region, sending the Baltis fleeing for their lives into the mountains to establish remote outposts like Hushe.

Here, in a low, smoky stone-and-mud hut with earthen floors, Gulam Rasool proudly welcomed me into his home. Rasool had been our cook during our time in the mountains. I'd liked him immediately and we'd become friends. He had lived with us at our base camp on the glacier for three months, working hard to keep us well fed in a cold and difficult place. Now his smile was white in the gloom of his hut. In the middle of the floor was a fire on which he and his wife cooked, and which was the only source of heat during the harsh winters. Smoke blackened the walls and clogged the air, making it hard to breathe. I was humbled.

Rasool was a diminutive Balti man, aged and wrinkled far beyond his 45 years and half-blinded by cataracts that grew across his eyes. But despite the ravages of time and his environment, he was a kind and gentle person, with a face that was a mirror to his emotions: I could tell exactly how he felt simply by looking at him. Rasool's smile came straight from his heart. He introduced his wife, who at 32 looked decades older, and his 13-year-old son, Ali. There had once been three children, but one had died in infancy and another, a son, had died when he was four years old, leaving them only with their beloved Ali. I sat in Rasool's threadbare home drinking smoky tea and I was happy because I could see how much joy his return had brought him.

Later, Rasool showed me around the village. The surrounding fields were beautiful in the late afternoon light, as golden wheat kernels washed themselves clean in the strong wind. Masherbrum stood tall at the head of the valley, a snowy, silent sentinel to this small village locked in the Himalaya. I could see the big glacier that we had painstakingly walked down two days previously. Rasool, half blind, somehow managing to pick his way down through the chaotic jumble of ice and rock, spurred on because he knew he was going home.

We crossed a Japanese-built wire suspension bridge over the river, which roared below the village, to reach their water powered grinding mill on the other side. Giant hand-hewn blocks of granite, worn smooth over hundreds of years, pulverised the precious wheat kernels into flour. Many generations had used the same medieval technology, and it still worked: water and stone turning wheat to flour, which was then turned into chapati bread so the village could eat. They live a tenuous existence in Hushe, dependent as they are on a short, fickle growing season for their subsistence, and on earning between US$6 and $30 a day for portering and cooking work on expeditions such as ours. In the autumn they have two short months of backbreaking labour to collect the harvest and process it before the first snow of winter cuts off the village. It's a hard life, the people look aged and used and even the children, with their cheeks rosily spotted by oxygen deficiency, look old beyond their years. Nothing much has changed there for centuries.

That afternoon in Hushe, I saw myself outside all margins, straddled between two cultures. I had left the conventions of my own society behind, and was peering into Rasool's. I suppose he was also square in the middle of his own page of unwritten rules, but the odd thing was I felt more at home in his world than my own. After we had paid our expedition staff, I had $8 left and a ticket back to the USA. I had no job to go back to, and nowhere to live, but I wasn't worried because those things always worked themselves out.

In their youth, Buddy and Dot had played by the rules and had found security without any freedom, I had the freedom without any security, and Rasool had neither, because neither bear relevance to his way of life and his limited options. He will never retire, even when he is old.

Even now, about once a year, I get a grimy, dog-eared letter from Rasool in the mail. I imagine him going to Mohammed Jaffar, the only man in Hushe who can write in English, and laboriously transcribing his letter. I can imagine the sticky taste of glue on Rasool's tongue and his calloused hands sealing the envelope shut and handing it over. Then the dusty Jeep ride, the letter passed from hand to hand, pocket to pocket, person to person from Hushe to Skardu to Islamabad to London, and then, eventually, to me. He writes to ask me when I will return, and he tells me about the expeditions on which he has worked and about having the cataracts removed from his eyes in Islamabad. The shaky handwriting tells me about his brothers, Mohammed and Ali Khan, who were our cooks on another trip, and about his son, Ali, who has started going with him on expeditions as his assistant and runner. And he asks that God keep me safe until we meet again.

I write back, telling him how I am and about my young son. I tell him how one day I will come and see him again and maybe I will bring my new family, and how I would like to go climbing there again. But what I don't write, and can't write, is how I have connected with him. I have connected with this simple rural man who lives on the other side of the earth and comes from a totally different culture and religion. I have the greatest respect for him because of his open, honest integrity and the things he values. I feel a far greater affinity for Rasool's world than Buddy's. Neither is better nor worse than the other, it's just that I can relate to the simplicity of Rasool's tightly knit community, his family, and the elemental life he leads in the endless cycle of seasons in Hushe. I have felt the harsh uncertainty of his life and tasted the raw edges because I have also been in a raw and uncertain place on the fringe. And it's only because I have looked out from the perimeters of both of our worlds that I could truly understand how much Rasool and I were essentially the same. Out on the margins, there really is no need for any book of rules. Pure survival is all that matters.

Rasool put it perfectly one evening while we were snowbound in our base camp high on the Goodwin-Austin glacier. A four-day storm had set in and it was dumping snow outside. Even the sporadic gunfire on the Siachen had stopped, as the Pakistani and Indian soldiers called off shelling each other in the bad weather. The pressure was off us, because we knew that we couldn't go up on the mountain tomorrow, or even the next day. Later, much later that night, long after the others had gone to bed, Rasool and I sat huddled in the kitchen tent under a belching kerosene lantern playing cards. I looked up, and his cloudy eyes met mine. "Have you had a good life, Rasool?" "Yes sahib, Inshallah, I will see my son grow up strong."

The Hour before Dawn

The alarm beeps far away, drawing you back from the surreal dreams of light sleep. Momentarily confused, your mind struggles to understand why you have been woken up at 2am on a cold, dark night. But that instant passes, and then you are all present. "Time to go, we have got to climb."

Tea is on and you scratch a few extra minutes warmth from the sleeping bag. It is like a tease: your body wants to stay warm and sleep, while your mind is bolt awake, planning action. The tea boils. You know how familiar it tastes, slightly metallic at altitude but sweet, and it always leaves you thirsty. A few mouthfuls of cereal, a slug of water, and you are out of your bag. The chill freezes your back as you lace up your boots and stuff the bag away. You shiver. You pack quickly. "Got to go, come on, got to go."

Breath frosts milky white in the frozen night air. You switch off the headlight for a moment and look at the stars, brilliant specks of white light in a black sky. But it is that huge, dark shape looming up there, where the stars are in shadow, that is pulling you.

That is why you are here, doing things one step at a time. "OK, ready?" You switch on the light and set off, stiffly at first. Your breath is ragged as you pull away, moving to get warm and find a rhythm. Your world has shrunk to the circle of light in front of you. After a few minutes your body warms and relaxes into a rhythm. Long, steady breaths, uphill, easy, your breathing becomes your movement and it grows effortless. You hear the squeak of crampons biting into hard frozen snow, and you see those little diamonds of ice crystals illuminated in the headlamp beam. The pack tugs your shoulders. You have been here before.

Your mind wanders as the movement takes over, thoughts drift – to people loved, and once loved – softly and silently in a dark and disconnected world. Everything is remote but at the same time very familiar. You could be anywhere, Peru, Patagonia, Chamonix, the Himalaya. Places change, but it is you who has remained more or less constant, that familiar strong body, strong breathing, pulling uphill in the same way. You know the chill on your face from the inevitable down-glacier wind that slices through your gloves as they hold the ice axe and ski pole.

And of course even the apprehension is the same, those old familiar doubts that bedevil you in the night. You worry about the weather, your speed, the conditions, the wind, the rockfall, the doubts, the tiny fears. Will we make it? Will we make it? You know that they always come and you have learned that the only way to dispel them is to go, to start up and then they just hang in the background because in front of you is ice and rock, and you have to concentrate hard. So there is no time for doubt and fear. Everything is right.

The slope drops away below you, the glacier a murky grey gloom in the darkness. You stop for a short rest and your breathing slows down, hard altitude breaths, dry and cold. Your back chills quickly from the wind as you sit on your pack and look at the stars, still firmly in night's grip. There is a certain time, about an hour before dawn, when you would swear that the stars surge slightly brighter, a momentary flash of sharper light. Perhaps it is their signal that they are on the wane. Perhaps it is an illusion caused by hypoxia, a shortage of oxygen.

But it is this hour before dawn that holds the most significance. Somehow it is colder and darker as the stars begin to fade after their flash. The hour passes slowly, even though your pace has quickened. You are even more isolated in your own small world. Doubts take on a sharper poignancy, as the black shape above you becomes nearer, bigger in your mind but smaller in the foreshortened blackness.

In the hour before dawn the wind seems to cut deeper than it had, but you are perfectly warm in the cold frozen night as long as you keep moving. Yes, this is your world. This is what you know and where you belong. You are comfortable here. You have heard this tune before and will doubtless hear it again, here where dark earth meets dark sky on the edge of dawn. And you are ready to climb. The first pale orange and gold seeps over the horizon, dawn is on its way and with it the sun and warm rock and high air and a glorious day. And you will be up there on that pale orange-and-grey wall when it changes to red as the sun ventures over the ridge. And you will be happy, free and alive, because this is your world, this beautiful alpine world.

An A to Z of Expedition Life

Answers to questions you always wanted to ask but were too afraid to …

A Ablutions. Privacy is not something you can be precious about when you're sharing a portaledge the size of a single bed. Any bodily functions are public knowledge and if you are on a well-climbed route you need to carry everything out with you, and I mean everything, using a pipe filled with kitty litter. In remote areas you can sling yourself to the wall and make use of all the space below. You can pee wherever you like, and sometimes on El Cap in Yosemite I would get lightly sprinkled by someone hundreds of metres above me.

B Bath. You don't wash very often, if at all. In the luxury of base camp a bucket of warm water heated on the stove, or a solar heated shower bag does the trick, but while climbing you don't wash. Fear not, you get used to it.

C Cooking. All cooking is done on a portable gas stove and fancy cuisine doesn't exist. We carry one small aluminium pot to be used for melting water, cooking a meal of instant pasta or noodles, and making tea. This single pot becomes the plate from which everyone eats and the only cutlery we bring is a spoon. Not much washing up goes on.

D Dirt. You get filthy. Your hair mats, your beard starts to itch and you begin to reek just a tad, but you didn't come to the mountains to look good. You don't have to be at your attractive best for your partner because they are in the same state.

E Equipment. Expedition climbing is all about freight management. You move literally tons of gear around the world, up the mountain and back again. While climbing, though, the ultimate aim is to take the bare essentials and to use everything in versatile ways. For example, an empty backpack placed over a looped rope becomes a mattress with your boots serving as a pillow.

F Food. What do we eat and drink up there?
Breakfast: a sachet of instant oatmeal and half a pot of tea.
Lunch: two energy bars.
Dinner: one packet of instant soup, one packet of instant noodles and half a pot of tea.
   Alpine climbing is an excellent way to go on diet without wanting or needing to.

G Gluttony. This occurs when the person you're with takes more than the exact half of food that is their share.

H Hunger. You're always hungry and fantasising about that huge stack of pancakes slathered in peanut butter, strawberry jam and maple syrup that you'll make when you get down.

I Irritation. Choose your partner carefully. Three months sharing a tent can feel like a very long time.

J Jokes. They're not that funny when you hear them for the third time.

K Knife. A Swiss army knife is essential for fixing small mechanical things that break, slicing food, and cutting your partner's rope.

(As happened to ill-fated climbing duo Simon Yates and Joe Simpson when they Touched the Void. See the next chapter for more detail on this misadventure.)

L Lights. Climbers almost always take a headlamp – except to Alaska in summer because it's light all night long. On alpine ice climbs it's best to start in the middle of the night while the ice is still frozen, before the sun softens it, causing rocks to fall on your head.

M Medicine in mountaineering is a serious topic. Injuries can be severe and wilderness first-aid is essential. You can't simply call for an ambulance, so self-sufficiency, a practical knowledge of basic trauma, and some medical supplies are key. Having said that, most climbers leave the first aid kit at base camp and venture onto the route with nothing at all.

N Night Naked is a phrase coined by Polish climber Voytek Kurtyka, to describe desperate blitz attacks on the highest peaks in the Himalaya with no equipment at all, no sleeping bags, no nothing. Only a tiny stove and some chocolate bars are allowed on these committing pursuit climbs done at night by headlamp. Daytimes, when it's warmer, are for resting.

O Organisation. The better organised you are, the more efficiently you can climb. They say that the best expeditions are planned on the back of an envelope but you can't leave anything behind so you have to plan very carefully. No matter how well organised you are, though, something will invariably go wrong.

P Portaledge. A sleeping platform for nights spent on big walls, a portaledge is very cramped but surprisingly comfortable. It's luxurious to lie down on a wall. You're always tied in to the rope, which is clipped into anchors in the rock, and you sleep in your harness, so despite looking precarious, you are quite safe.

Q Quick. The speed at which you get out of the way when things start falling on you.

R Relaxation. Before and after climbing we chill out completely, sleep a lot, read books, play cards, or do nothing at all. Rest days are important to prepare for the intense bursts of action to come.

S Sex. None. It's too cold and you don't want to get out of your sleeping bag. Besides, in the big mountains you invariably have an altitude-induced headache.

T Teeth. When you're climbing alpine routes you don't take a toothbrush and toothpaste because it's an unnecessary extra. Fuzziness is part of the game, like storms and falling rocks. But on wall climbs, where you're hauling a ton of equipment, food and water anyway, you can bring such small creature comforts.

U Underwear. No you don't bring a change of underwear. You make do. Some British climbers have a tradition of burning them when they get down.

V Vegetables and fresh greens are sorely lacking. To ward off the nasty effects of scurvy a lot of climbers supplement their diet with multivitamin tablets.

W Water. In the snow and ice there is plenty of water, but it's all frozen. A small gas stove is therefore essential for survival. Everything you drink has to be melted on the stove, which takes time. It is an indescribable luxury to return from the mountains, turn on a tap and take a drink.

X Xtra Careful. You have to be exceptionally careful because if you drop anything it falls a long way. Take for example the American, Mark Twight, and his Canadian climbing partner, Barry Blanchard, who dropped their ropes halfway up the monstrous

3000-metre Rupal Face on Nanga Parbat, Pakistan, which meant they had to climb all the way down the ice face to retrieve them - unroped. Luckily for them they found, by chance, an abandoned haulbag left by a Japanese team, which contained some ropes with which they could continue their descent in safety.

Y Yes! What you say when you get invited to go on an expedition. Overdrafts, work commitments and family can be sorted out later.

Z zzz Sleep. One of the qualities necessary for a good alpinist is that you are able to sleep anywhere. Sometimes accommodation can be significantly less than palatial, and often you have to sleep sitting up, and sometimes even standing up. But if you're tired enough it won't matter where you sleep.

The Dru

A few kilometres beyond Chamonix on the road to Argentiere one passes through the Bois de Favre, a dense forest of silver pines. Suddenly the trees end at a clearing: the rocky terminal moraine marking the end of the once extensive glacier, the Mer de Glace (Sea of Ice), which had carved its way steadily to this point under millions of tons of ice. If one looks up from here, and it's hard not to, especially if you're a climber, it's the one place along the Arveyon valley that the full immensity of the Petit Dru can be seen. The West Face rises out of the timberline, wild and jagged, for thousands of metres, before gradually tapering to a slender needlepoint silhouette that pierces the pale blue sky. It's an almost perfect granite spire.

The Dru is the fullstop at the end of a nine-kilometre serrated ridge of great geological tension, which starts at Mont Dolent, with its feet on the borders of France, Switzerland and Italy. The ridge sweeps westward over the jagged heads of the Triollet, Courtes, Droites,

Aiguille Verte, and the Grand Dru, before suddenly ending with a heart-stopping drop over the edge of the Petit Dru. From there this gruelling spine of shattered, unstable alpine geography dribbles down the arête of the Flammes de Pierre, into the Mer de Glace, but its power has worn out by then, stolen by the West Face of the Petit Dru.

When I first saw the Dru I wanted it – all of it. Like an addict, I wanted to climb every route on that beautiful slender spire. I wanted to possess it, to have it, to have done it, and to make it mine. Like a compulsive gambler slipping coins into slots, an irredeemable alcoholic, or a paedophile lusting after an underage Lolita, I couldn't get enough of this steep, shadowy rock wall with its alternating orange buttresses and dark grey dihedrals. Instead of women, money or drink, my hands caressed sharp granite as the air dropped away beneath my feet. The Dru was my Aphrodite of mountains: the archetype of beauty and mountaineering perfection. Not only did the Dru have a tall, slender elegance, but it was also hard to win over, with tough technical climbs on all sides and no easy route to the top. That's what I believe real climbing is all about, a beautiful peak that is a challenge to climb.

Driven by my desire to possess the Dru, I ended up climbing most of its routes, covering many thousands of metres, climbing and descending, admiring at close quarters the fineness of its pale orange cracks and long grey corners. And sometimes suffering its whims: the snow, the ice and the bad bivouacs. And yet, despite my infatuation, it isn't the climbing or the Dru itself that I remember, so much as the people with whom I climbed and with whom I shared those intense moments, especially Jarda; driven and ill-fated.

Nothing about the Dru is constant, and neither have been the lives of the people I met and befriended in my time there. So this is a story of love and loss and life in the mountains.

The Dru itself has suffered catastrophic losses. All of us who have climbed there have experienced first hand the terrible clatter and whistle of the daily rock falls, the natural results, they say, of exfoliation's freeze and thaw cycles, perfectly normal for such a young set of mountains. But I think that global warming is taking its toll. In

1997 most of the central part of the West Face exploded off, crashing down and utterly changing a wall we'd known so well. Four years later, while climbing the Plan des Aguilles in 2001, I looked back at it and didn't recognise any of the features. All I saw was a long grey scar. The fantastic red pillar of the French Direct, a route that had cleaved the wall for half of its height and that I'd climbed alone, had gone. The pillar lay buried under thousands of tons of rubble on the Dru Glacier far below. And then on 29 June 2005 the upper part of the West Face and the Bonatti Pillar came crashing down, altering the skyline profile of the Dru forever.

In only 20 years, I've seen glaciers retreat, the winter snowfall drop to half of what it used to be, and the hotter summers bake the already unstable rock and melt the ice. The Alps are much drier now. And this acceleration has all culminated at the flash point of the West Face of the Dru. Three times in the last 20 years the mountain has shed its skin like a monstrous geological reptile, each time leaving a new facade of fragile, loose, pale grey rock.

It was a while before I met Jarda. My first foray on the Dru was with Welshman Mick Hardwick. Long, lean and supple on the rock and searingly witty in the pub, I joined Mick on the classic Chamonix test piece, the climb up the American Direct to the Jammed Block. Once up there I was sorely tempted to continue to where a feature called The 90-metre Dihedral beckoned strongly, but we hadn't come prepared for that. And I had had a good foretaste of the seductive pleasures of the Dru.

A year later, I joined Mick for several weeks' climbing in the UK. Mick had a feisty, understated, typically restrained British demeanour. While climbing the classic route, Strawberries, at Tremadog in Wales, I watched in bemusement as he held onto the minuscule holds for dear life, using every ounce of his strength, his eyes bugging out with the effort and the determination not to give in. Long after his exhausted arms had worn out, sheer, bloody-minded will-power kept him hanging on. He fought and fought and eventually pulled himself over the top. All he said afterwards, with a sly grin, was: "Good, innit?" Over climbs at Pembroke, Gogarth and Llanberis Pass, and pints of tea at

Pete's Café in Llanberis, we sealed our friendship. Mick was a professional guide, and he was planning a trip to Pumori in the Himalayas in the autumn, after a summer working for the International School of Mountaineering in Switzerland. I was planning to return to the Alps for as long as it took. I shook his big hand goodbye in Gwynedd in Wales. And never saw him again. He caught the Twin Otter in Nepal, from Kathmandu to Lukla, en route to Pumori, but the plane never got there. Apparently the engines failed. All they found were some melted climber's carabiners in the smouldering wreckage deep in the tangled undergrowth of the Dhud Khosi gorge. Mick was 26 years old.

The ghosts of the Dru, and their stories and legends continued to haunt me. The minute I returned to Chamonix, I knew exactly what I wanted to do. I wanted to solo the Bonatti Pillar; to climb it alone, just like the legendary Italian first ascentionist, Walter Bonatti, my childhood hero, had done 32 years earlier. Except that by now the route was well known and well travelled and it took me two days instead of a week, as I roped every pitch calmly and methodically, and bivouacked 12 pitches up on an excellent ledge beneath an overhang. It was one pitch below the remains of the ledge on which the accident-prone British climber, Joe Simpson, along with his fellow Brit, Ian Whittaker, had been sleeping when the whole ledge collapsed beneath them. There they were, one moment sleeping peacefully and the next the ground literally dropped from underneath them in a horrifying moment of bad luck and bad judgement, leaving them hanging off a crumbling flake without boots or any equipment in the pitch darkness. And there they hung for 12 harrowing hours before they were finally rescued. After that Joe Simpson would go on to have traumatic epics and narrow escapes the world over, culminating in his infamous experience on Siula Grande in Peru.

Vividly documented in his international best seller *Touching the Void*, Joe had broken his leg high on the mountain in a fall off a ridge, which lead to a desperate descent, sliding down the snowy slopes rope length by rope length in tricky weather conditions. Until suddenly, out of sight and earshot of his climbing partner, Simon Yates, he shot over a cliff and hung suspended in space. After an hour, Simon, not knowing what had happened to Joe, was forced to cut the rope, sending Joe plummeting into a crevasse. Which might have been the end of the story had Joe not been of such a pugnacious personality. Left for dead, he crawled his way out of the crevasse and down to their base camp, laying the tracks for what would become a story of pure survival. But all of that was yet to come as I sat on my ledge below theirs and wondered idly why they had chosen to bivouac there at all. The full white moon rose over the Tafelere Glacier following a deep purple sunset and I looked out over the wilderness of rock and ice and thought, "Yes, this is the place I want to be." I reached the summit easily the next day.

I also fell in love with Julie on the Dru. I met her the day after I had solo climbed up the French Direct, a little-climbed route that had first been climbed four years prior by the Frenchman Christophe Profit. She requested a climbing partner, but she would become so much more. Her words marked the start of a long relationship and a lifelong friendship. One of the first routes we did together was the North Face of the Dru. After a day of treacherous mixed climbing in poor conditions, we bivvied at the top of The Niche. Just before dark I walked to the edge of the West Face and peered over. A thousand metres of steep granite plunged straight down onto the Dru Rognon below. Not far from where I stood I saw a rusty old bolt, and knew immediately that it had been put there by Gary Hemming. These mountains are suffused with so much history. Hemming was an American expatriate living in Europe, an alternative and very talented hippie who had made the first ascent of the American Direct. He had rappelled from this point in 1963 on a dramatic rescue to assist injured French climbers long before helicopters or the Secours de Montagne (French Mountain Rescue) could rescue you from pretty much anywhere in the Alps. Hemming was depressed and a little bit crazy. He eventually shot himself in Wyoming the year I was born, but I have no doubt that the Dru had captivated him just as it had captivated me. Julie and I carried on to reach the summit the following afternoon in the mist. There was no wide vista of the Jorasses, the Midi or the Chamonix

Aguilles, only a dim awareness of the bulk of the Grand Dru lurking in the cloud just behind us. It was my fourth trip to the summit in two months. My thirst for the Dru had almost been slaked.

There must have been a certain irony in the fact that I first ran into Jarda on the Dru. At the time I was with Dave Litch, a patriotic Scotsman and a fine climbing partner, and we were slowly hiking up from Montenvers bound for American Direct, so that we could continue on the route from where Mick and I had left off. Dave was an aspirant guide and a dapper mountain man. He was a good friend too. We'd climbed winter ice on Ben Nevis and shared a doss in London, but this would be one of our last outings. That winter Dave was killed while skiing in the Cairngorms in the eastern Scottish Highlands when a slab avalanche overtook him. Nowadays, whenever I hear Mark Knopfler's song 'On Every Street', it reminds me of Dave, the street-smart cad he had once been. Another young life was cut short by the snow. Dave was 25 years old.

But that day we knew none of this as we laboured up the slope and spotted two weary climbers coming down. They were clearly East European. After a while you can guess the nationality of climbers in the Alps just by looking at them, their gear and their clothing. What gave these guys away were their striped tracksuit pants. Only Communist Bloc climbers wore striped tracksuit pants. They had that slightly dazed and disappointed air, which we immediately recognised as a look that said that they had had an epic, or a struggle, or they hadn't managed to summit a route. I later learned that they'd had an epic in the Dru couloir and they had failed to climb the route because the midsummer ice was melting while they were climbing, and water was running down the couloir.

Some weeks after that, Jarda appeared at our camp in Pierre D'Orthaz selling down jackets and titanium ice screws. He was a big man with soaring Slavic cheekbones, red cheeks, and a physique perfectly suited to carrying huge packs in the mountains. Joze 'Jarda' Rozman was Czechoslovakian and he spoke very little English, but I saw fire and determination in his eyes. It's hard to miss when you recognise your own kind. I saw big mountains in his future.

A leap of faith. Every BASE jump is a stimulating mix of judgement and luck, especially from the white rock of The Lookout on Table Mountain, the margins are slim.

35

36

Best friend and wife for nine years, Julie and I shared a world into which I could have ventured with few others. She loved the mountains, no matter how tough, and I loved being there with her.

37

38

39

40

Together Julie and I roamed the world seeking big spaces and high mountains. The lovely ridge above is approaching 5000 metres, on the West Buttress, Denali in Alaska. Over nearly a decade of marriage we slept in some pretty odd places.

With a grubbiness matched only by their enthusiasm, The Technicals watched our every move on the hot and dusty Rhumsiki Tower in Cameroon.

43

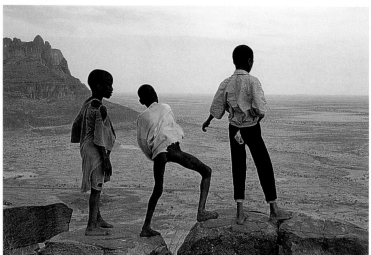

44

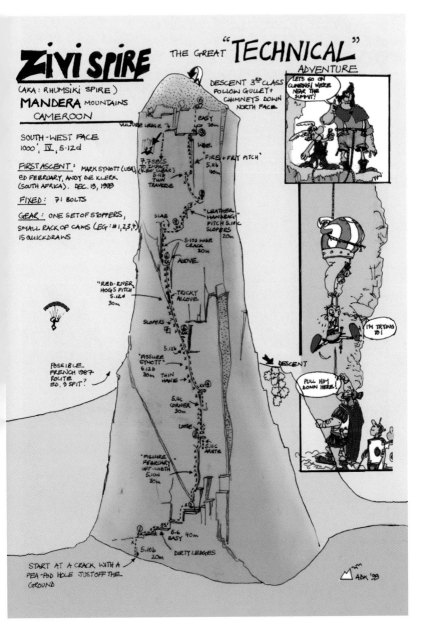

46

For a long time I was infatuated with
the spiky peaks of the Alps, the Eiger
(left and right) and the Dru (above).
I also loved Rodney, the temperamental
dream car that got me there.

47

48

For 20 years Milner Peak was my nemesis. Deep in the Hex River Mountains, many climbers and BASE jumpers believe that there is more of a hex to the place than just the river. On these walls gravity becomes a fearsome force.

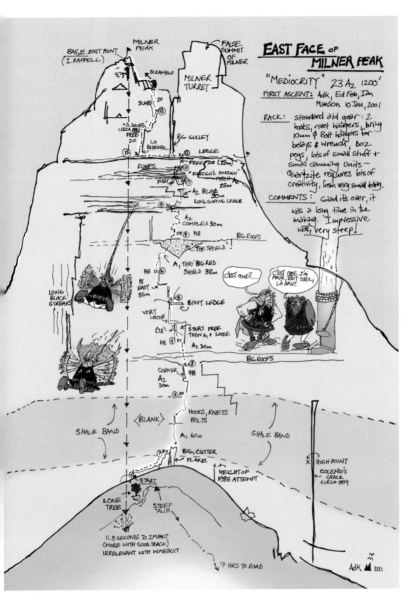

At long last, after loads of struggle and big air, Ed and I completed the climb on Milner and I could draw a topo of the route for future climbers. I hope they fare better than these characters from Asterix.

53

Milner Peak: Squashed onto a portaledge, high above the ground, it's lucky Ed and I are good friends. In BASE jumping you are all alone, whatever happens.

Not quite a bird, not totally human either, flying wingsuits from Milner Peak is an intoxicating thrill.

There is something that sets Eastern Bloc alpinists apart from the rest of us. In an article entitled 'Between the Hammer and the Anvil', the Australian mountaineer and writer Greg Child examined their phenomenal success. He argued that after all the bartering, trading, fiddling and scheming it took to break through the Iron Curtain, the consequences of failure on a route in the West were huge, unthinkable. Climbing success was their ticket to freedom. They couldn't fail, so they went for it, consequences be damned. With their backs up against the wall, a whole generation of Eastern Bloc climbers did some of the boldest ascents ever in big mountains all over the world. It also wiped out nearly all of them. As Westerners, most of us were wimps in comparison. I saw this kind of resolve in Jarda's eyes. But I didn't buy anything from him, although unbeknownst to both of us it wouldn't be long before I would be the one twisting those same titanium screws into hard winter ice.

I next bumped into him as I entered Snell Sports in Chamonix, stamping the snow from my boots as the fug of central heating instantly warmed my face. The wide plate–glass windows looked onto leaden grey skies, thick snow and deep February winter outside. And there was Jarda, red cheeks glowing in the warmth. His English was still nonexistent, and his French not much better. "*Escalade?*" (Climb?) "*Oui.*" (Yes) And it was sealed. A few days later we clipped into our skis and glided down the Vallée Blanche, a popular ski descent with hoards of other skiers, but after a while we turned off and broke away from the crowds to traverse below the Dent Blanche and up to The Shroud on the Grandes Jorrasses. Together, using sign language, we climbed that long sheet of ice with our skis strapped to our packs. Jarda was like a bullet. Once he'd aimed himself at the top of something, there was almost nothing that could stop his trajectory, and somehow we connected on this fundamental, almost primeval level, despite our inability to communicate. Over the summit we dropped down into Italy to hitchhike back through the Mont Blanc tunnel to Chamonix. Neither of us had Italian visas, but why do you need a visa if you're leaving the country anyway? This was just a warm-up. Next we were to tackle the Dru.

Until then Jarda had been camping in the snow, more or less living out of a van with some Slovakian friends of his and spending most of the time skiing. He was a really good skier. I secured him an occasional warm berth and a place to dry out gear at the already overcrowded apartment of Gary Kinsey, a British friend of mine who had rented a tiny place in Chamonix. There was never any room to sleep, which was usually impossible anyway due to the frequent parties and countless visitors from the UK.

Jarda liked to go into the Chamonix supermarkets, climbing stores and hardware shops just to look, not just at the vast array of shiny consumer goods available, but also at the boxes and boxes of stocks packed on the shelves. He said very little, but his eyes said it all. Perhaps it was because he couldn't speak our language, but he always looked haunted and hungry and resolute: a distant, self-contained man when he was with us. But when I saw him with his friends, he was voluble and animated, sounding off in Slovak, which sounded a lot like trying to talk English with his mouth full. I don't know where he came from or anything about his family, but he was a good climber and he had done a lot of routes in Chamonix. We were going through the guidebook one evening and I pointed to a picture of the Dru couloir and on impulse asked, *"Tu ver faire, Jarda?"* (Want to do it?). His blue eyes lit up and he cracked a wide toothy grin. *"Oui."* We kept an eye on the weather and waited for a good forecast. When it came, we packed for the Dru couloir in the corridor of our crowded flat as drunken Swedes stepped over our gear. His food contribution was *saucisson* (sausage), cheese and powdered soup, which, come to think of it, was all I ever saw him eat. He even ate soup and meat for breakfast.

From the Grandes Montets cable station high on the flank of the Dru, we waded through deep snow down to the Nant Blanc glacier. The day was crispy blue and cold, clean and white like a glittering fairytale. We crossed under the Aiguille Sans Nom and finally the couloir came into view, a narrow gash splitting the North Face. It was the first time I'd seen it properly. The ice was thick, white and very steep. The whole of the Dru was plastered. It looked amazing.

"OK?" "OK." Jarda burrowed through the Bergschrund, the split in the ice between the glacier and the mountain, and climbed into the couloir itself, which ran like a vertical gorge from the mountain's summit to the base. He was rock solid on ice and very strong. It was a pleasure to climb with someone like that. We talked in broken French and English, and although sign language was more effective, we really didn't need to say much because we both knew what we were doing. The first three pitches were very delicate, thin, plate ice over slabs and above that the couloir opened up as we climbed up loose powder snow sprinkled over hard ice towards the Breche where the real climbing began. As we progressed we became part of that cold blue-and-white world. The ice was brittle, each blow of the axe fracturing the ice and sending it raining down onto the belayer, freezing quietly below. The couloir narrowed. The climbing was steep, mixed, exhilarating and technical because of the blanket of dry powder snow that covered everything, but there were plenty of opportunities to find gear placements if you dug beneath the snow. The rock walls closed in on either side.

At mid-afternoon we reached the crux of the route, the Fissure Nominee, and it looked desperate. A 10-centimetre mantle of ice choked the vertical crack, it was too thin to ice climb, and too thick to rock climb. A few metres above the belay I managed to hang precariously and twist an ice screw into the ice, but as I got it halfway in, the ice splintered, turning the screw into a dodgy cam instead. I was getting more and more pumped, so I hung doggedly on it and miraculously it held. "*Allez*, good", came the encouragement from Jarda waiting in the shadows below me in his overstuffed down parka. I carried on up in this manner – some free moves, some aid – butchering the ice in the crack because we didn't have the right size gear, and I eventually reached the belay which was an old peg at a ledge just big enough to stand on. Hours had flown by and the day had vanished. Grey wispy clouds streaked the sky and the Nant Blanc ridge briefly flared purple as night settled onto us with a deep blue hush. Jarda followed as I scanned the gloom above. All I could see was steep ice, and everything below was even steeper. Bivouac prospects looked bleak. I knew we were in for a long and grisly night.

It was pitch dark when he arrived at the belay, covered in snowy spindrift with ice encrusting his face. "Bivvy here, OK?" "OK." We each retreated into our own worlds as we prepared for the night. I rigged a suspended platform that I could sit on using my pack, my axes and some slings and draped myself saddle-like into my horse for the night. My sleeping bag came up to my waist and my one leg kept falling asleep, but at least I managed to get my boots off. Jarda fashioned something similar and we both half hung, half sat and half stood as the night froze hard. Jarda gnawed on a frozen hunk of *saucisson* and balanced the stove on a shelf of rock with his hands while we made a brew and some soup, which we slurped straight from the pot. Afterwards I looked at my watch. It was only nine o'clock.

The night was interminable. It was impossible to get comfortable. At first I thought he had gone to sleep, but when Jarda started humming and talking to himself in Slovakian I knew he wasn't as impervious to cold as he looked. When the cold got too bad we rubbed our arms and legs to try to get some circulation going. The lights of Chamonix twinkled in another world far below us as we dozed and thrashed and wriggled and shook and shivered. The wind came up and blew spindrift onto us and the cold, clear, starry night sucked all the warmth out of us. It was a night I'll never forget.

It took an age to get going in the grey light of morning. Jarda had a strained, pinched look from the cold and the sleepless night as he led off on the next section. The rush of blood to my hands was excruciating after I finally started moving, but I did warm up and as luck would have it, there was a decent ledge just a pitch higher around the corner to the right. One more tricky crack with a few aid moves put us onto thicker solid ice as the couloir continued relentlessly upwards. Eventually the angle eased slightly and opened up to easier ground. We climbed up cracks and over blocks, struggling to find our way because everything was covered in clingy loose powder snow. But we reached the summit, under a sky that had become veiled with cloud. I felt very isolated standing there on top of the Dru, so far from home, in a cutting wind that was a forerunner of the approaching storm. The world was sharp, jagged and white as far as I could see. We spent less than a minute on top.

They leave a section of the Charpoa Hut open in winter for people like us. It's a dark mountain hovel and there was ice on the floor, but to us it seemed like paradise. Jarda found two cases of one-and-a-half litre Orangina soft drink bottles in the hut storeroom that had been stashed away for the following summer. They were frozen solid, but we made orange flavoured pasta and fell asleep warm, flat and comfortable. It was snowing the next day as Jarda loaded up his 20 bottles of frozen Orangina and we waded down through deep snow to the Mer de Glace and then down the trail to Chamonix under pines laden thick and heavy with snow. Near the bottom Jarda started laughing as a skier caught an edge of a ski and wiped out in front of us. We were both glad to get down.

"OK, Jarda?"

"OK."

"*C'est bien?*" (All is well?)

"*Oui.* Is good. Good climb."

We had spent a total of seven days tied into a rope together, without being able to speak much of the other's language, but that didn't matter at all. Sometimes with climbing you can simply click with a partner in a way that doesn't need words. I felt an affinity for the big, unshaven man with strength to spare ploughing through the snow in front of me. And even though I hardly knew him, he had made a big impression on me.

I had finished with the Dru. My desire had been slaked at last.

I don't know where Jarda ended up, but I did hear via the grapevine that he had taken on a job doing some of the most horrible work imaginable: cleaning out the inside of tanker trucks. He would be lowered down inside with a respirator and a light and he would pressure wash, sandblast and repaint the inside of the tanks.

Jarda was killed in 1994 on Kangchenjunga, while attempting the huge and treacherous Southwest Face alpine style, a bold and dangerous attempt. Apparently the whole slope they were climbing avalanched near the summit. They didn't have a chance.

Jarda is gone. I sometimes wonder where he would be now if he were still alive, but perhaps his destiny and the big mountains had been locked together right from the start.

There is no doubt that in the years to come routes will be climbed or reclimbed on the 'new' Dru, and these in turn will add another layer of legend to a mountain already rich in history and effort. Time has moved on. Like flicking through a book, in one sweep a whole chapter has gone. Walter Bonatti is an old man now. I never met him although he inspired me, just as he inspired countless other young alpinists with his simple message to climb beautiful lines on hard peaks. The Bonatti Pillar, one of his masterpieces, has gone, but in the end it doesn't matter. We spent our youth chasing dreams, and we found them, on the Dru and elsewhere. If alpinism is a form of poetry, then the mountains onto which we wrote our lives were just transient pages. Except that in the case of the Dru we certainly didn't expect such dramatic changes in our lifetime. It was a mountain after all, something that should have been far more permanent than ourselves and when the rock of stability finally crumbles all it does is highlight the transience of our lives.

I loved being on the Dru. I loved the raw mountain power that the peak exuded. I loved the wildness, the steepness and the history of all of those who had been there before. I loved the rough alpine granite beneath my fingers and the blue shadows of early mornings on the wall. I feel a sadness for my friends who shared it with me, not because they are gone, but because of all the life they missed in the future.

Life goes on. It always does. And it always turns out in the end.

Stages of Men

MY FIRST-BORN

I saw you take your first breath as you came into the world, all curled up and bloody like a little sausage. Then the midwife handed me a pair of scissors, and as I cut your cord with a squeaky, rubbery snip, tears stinging my eyes and a throat that felt like it had swallowed an apple whole, you became a separate human being. Separate from your mother. You were alive, a perfectly formed new person. It was little short of a miracle.

Later that night, as your mother slept away the pain and tiredness, you slept on my chest, my newborn son, a tiny snuffling bundle wrapped up tightly with eyes clamped shut. I talked to you while you slept. I told you about the four stages of being a man: the youth, the warrior, the head of the household, and the final contemplation. That night we each moved along a place, you became a youth and I became the head of a brand new family.

I told you about my father and my mother. I told you about my childhood and then I told you about all the places I had been: about rock and snow and mountains and cold nights and high places and what it feels like to fall through the air. I told you about the people I loved and my regrets and joys and hopes, and I told you about how very glad I was to be here, still in this world. And what it feels like to be your brand new dad.

I talked, softly, but you didn't hear me, and it didn't matter because what I was saying wouldn't have been heard anyway. I was telling you about all the sorrows and mistakes and pitfalls that I had fallen into. You are going to go through it all yourself anyway. But that's what wisdom is, a distillation of the bare truths in the life we have to live and you can only get there by doing it yourself.

After they'd washed the blood of birth off you and I held you for the first time, all red and wrinkled and squashed and covered in vernix, I felt in a flash the circle of my own life closing, as yours had only just opened. I suddenly felt unconditional love: I would be there for you and do whatever it took to nurture you, care for you and help you, for the rest of my life. I suddenly felt from the heart, rather than intellectually, what our wedding vows really meant. There was no longer just me and your mother as separate people. Our family was now connected forever in blood, real blood, your blood, our blood. Your birth was carnal, but it all came together in that instant: the moment when flesh and emotion turned into pure joy. Words can't even come close to describing how I felt as I held you for the first time, because it was just pure love.

I could hardly believe that a human could be so tiny. Your little hand clutched onto my finger: five perfect fingers with nails as small as pinheads. I looked at your hands and I wondered what those hands would do. Would they latch onto small handholds on steep cliffs like mine? Or would they dip into salty ocean water, propelling a surfboard into a wave like your mother's? Would these hands tap away at a computer keyboard, turn the pages of books or hold a scalpel, a rifle, helicopter controls or nothing but air as they skydive from dizzy heights? Would they move paper or would they weld metal? Would they design rockets, fit pipes, or play the violin? Or would these hands shake as they beg for small change while they prepare a needle on a dirty city street corner? Will these hands ever hold a little child in the years to come, or will they die holding a machine gun in the corner of a foreign field in another ill-conceived war?

Your life and the path it takes are yours to decide. I'll show you my world and I'll show you my values, but then it's all up to you. I'll be there for you whatever you decide. And all I can really do beyond that is hope for your happiness, good health, and that fate will be kind to you.

I can't even imagine what your life will hold because of all of the limitless possibilities and the boundless choices that lie before you. The world is yours, my son. Your tiny legs will first walk, and I'll hold your hand when you take those first steps. Then you'll run, and I'll run with you. And then your legs will take you off into the world, maybe to the far ends of the earth if that's what you want, and I'll watch, and be there when you come back. If you come back.

Winter's dawn crept softly into the room. You started cackling, a newborn cry, and it was time to wake mom and put you onto her breast. It was time for you to suckle and feed, and start on your long journey of growing strong and growing up and then going out into the world. And then, maybe one day, when you're ready, of having a child of your own and starting a new circle. If you do, then you'll know what I've been talking about, about what it means to love someone completely, and about how it feels to grow up and pass on the flame of youth.

The Great Technical Adventure

The movie was a classic French art film, *Chocolat*, and the young actress absolutely gorgeous. She was petite, dark haired, and she wasn't wearing a thing under her flimsy white dress. I sat in the darkened movie theatre transfixed. But I wasn't looking at her, or paying much attention to the plot, because in the background bizarre rock towers rose out of thorn-scrub hills like sheer, stony-brown fingers. They resembled something out of a Tolkien novel, but to me the fantasy didn't stretch that far because I could see they were climbable. So I sat there and waited and waited until the last of the credits rolled up to the words "Filmed on location in Cameroon". The seed had been planted. I had to go there.

Nine years after watching that film, Ed and I finally got to go to Cameroon, to see those towers and experience them first hand. It was while we were fishing around for funding that an American friend of ours, Mark Synott, e-mailed back to say he was keen to join us. Mark, at 28, was a veteran adventure climber, having done ascents of new routes on some of the biggest walls in the world, in Pakistan, Baffin Island in the Canadian Arctic, Yosemite in USA and Patagonia on the far tip of South America.

Mark is tall, dark and handsome in the classic American sense, someone who could have been a movie star if he didn't like climbing and exploring so much, and he has a persuasive personality to match. So, without much difficulty, he talked National Geographic

Television into funding an expedition to climb in Cameroon and make a documentary film. Although at the time we had very little idea of what the towers would be like. Our only references were the vague black-and-white photos that we'd pulled off the Internet, which ensured that we knew nothing of the rock quality, the exact size of the walls, their precise location or their feasibility for climbing. But National Geographic TV was very excited by the project and the budget blossomed, which was fine by us because it's always nice to go on trips paid for by someone else. We arranged to meet in Cameroon early in December 1999.

Ed and I knew little about the country other than it was home to the indomitable Cameroon Lions, the national soccer team. But we quickly learned all about their national airline. The weekly flight on Cameroon Airlines from Johannesburg was scheduled to depart at 9am. At five to nine, after waiting in a queue for over two hours, we eventually reached the check-in desk and I politely asked the attendant what time the flight was actually leaving.

"Nine am," she replied breezily and walked off, her watch clearly set on Africa time. We ended up leaving in the early afternoon. Cameroon airlines, with its lone Boeing 737, was to become the bane of our lives.

Many, many hours later, after unannounced, unscheduled and sweltering four-hour stops in Kinshasa in the Democratic Republic of the Congo, and Brazzaville directly across the Congo River in the neighbouring Congo Republic, we finally arrived in Douala, Cameroon's largest city. Douala is disparagingly and quite appropriately known as the armpit of Africa because it's ringed by equatorial jungle on three sides and it lies cradled in the crook of Africa, right where the coastline turns sharply westwards towards the Ivory Coast. It is a seriously sweaty place.

At the airport we met up with Mark and the rest of our team. National Geographic's plan was for Ed, Mark and me to play starring roles in a sober documentary that would be filmed by my long-time friend from Seattle, the Australian mountaineer and writer, Greg Child. Greg is probably the best all-round climber in the world. He's climbed Everest, K2 and Gasherbrum IV, done first ascents of big walls around the world, and is an excellent rock climber to boot. Along with these stellar credentials, he is also the funniest and most irreverent person I know, with a sharp, gutter wit honed in the Sydney climbing culture. Greg and Mark knew each other well from past climbs. Greg's fond nickname for Mark was "Ballsack", while Mark called Greg "The Old Leather Handbag", because the sunburnt, reptilian skin on the back of Greg's neck looked, admittedly, a lot like leather at close inspection. The two of them kept up an ongoing verbal sparring match, ripping everybody to shreds continuously and making us laugh until our sides ached. In contrast, the last two team members were rather more serious. Simon Boyce, the producer and director for the film, was the proper Englishman, immaculately mannered and less forthcoming than our more ribald companions, and Robin Freeman, a pretty young American woman, was the coordinator. Robin had lived in West Africa for several years, first as a Peace Corps worker, and then as a manager for all of National Geographic's expeditions to the region. She knew how to get around, who to bribe, and she spoke perfect French which was essential. With such a motley cast and crew, our project promised to be a fun and exciting adventure.

But things went awry almost immediately, thanks to our friends at Cameroon Airlines who'd lost all my baggage. Everything. I found myself about to embark on a climbing expedition with no gear what-soever, bar a pair of flip-flops and a BASE-jumping parachute that I had carried with me into the cabin. The extensive medical kit and vast supplies of food that Ed and I had so carefully prepared after learning our lesson in Mali the year before was missing. After a brief caucus we calculated that among us we had enough gear to be able to do some climbing and I decided that I would buy a blanket and a pair of tennis shoes to equip me for the expedition. The rest I could share or borrow. The blanket I found at a street market – it was scratchy but serviceable – and the shoes came from a sports shop. They were the spitting image of a well-known brand until you looked closely. And they fell apart after the first week.

Outside the airport the muggy heat hit me like a solid cloak of dripping humidity. We set off into the heavy night, just as Joseph

Conrad had done a century previously, hoping that this were not to be our heart of darkness.

But our journey that night took us as far as the five-star Douala Intercontinental Hotel, where Ed, Greg, Mark and I lounged around the pool sipping cocktails for three days while Robin wrestled with Cameroon Airlines to try to book us tickets to the northern part of the country. Five stars in Cameroon equates to a two-star hotel anywhere else, but it was clean and comfortable. Ed settled back into his poolside lounger, cracked open another cold beer, and said, "You know lads, I think I could get into this African exploration stuff in a big way."

Robin pulled all the strings she could and bribed the right people, and on day four we boarded a flight to Garoua, the closest city to our destination in the Mandara Mountains in the extreme north of Cameroon, where it borders Nigeria and Chad. We were on our way, or so we thought. But once airborne, the intercom rattled into life and the pilot announced that we wouldn't be going to Garoua anymore, but to N'djamena in Chad instead. After landing there, we took off again, this time destined for a town called Maroua, where we were unceremoniously kicked out, even though we had paid to go to Garoua. By now all of us had had quite enough of Cameroon Airlines and we willingly debunked to travel the rest of the way by bus and Jeep.

Finally, eight days after leaving South Africa, we chugged up a rough track in the evening light and caught sight of the towers. They were beautiful and haunting. They seemed desolate and stoically resigned to their fate as lonely sentinels standing guard over dry savanna and scattered acacia on the fringes of the great Sahara desert. Our banter hushed up, and for once even Greg was silent. There is something about the African continent that captures people's souls, and to me this other-worldly landscape explained it. Africa is ancient and primal and these stark volcanic plugs, which had stood immutable and steadfast like sentries against time itself, were testimony to that as the rest of the earth had simply eroded away around them. Africa feels really old, and it affected us all, sitting silently awe-struck in the Jeep. Silently awe-struck that is, until Greg piped up in his ripe Aussie accent: "Just look at them, they've all got hard-ons."

As we made our camp just outside the small village of Rhumsiki, an old man with tired eyes hung his sickle across his bony shoulders and watched us for a while. Time paused. The Kapsiki mountain people live in this region, and all around us were neatly tended millet fields. The village itself was a loose conglomeration of round mud bungalows and corrugated-iron shacks. It was pretty far off the beaten track, but it had a school, a clinic and piped water all supplied by UN Aid. The local people seemed in relatively good health and the village itself was neat and orderly, quite unlike the filthy squalor of Douala. The old man slowly returned to his labours and time resumed.

No sooner had we started to pitch our tents than our camp flooded with curious young boys, aged between six and 12, who squatted on the perimeters and watched our every move, like the vultures that circled the towers high above us. Greg nicknamed them the "Technicals" after he'd made a joke about child soldiers and the Somali private militias riding through the streets of Mogadishu in armoured pick-up trucks. Later they would become our own private army. We got to know a few of them after a while. They were strong boys who had to grow up quickly in that part of the world.

We had run into a small problem, literally. The towers weren't nearly as big as we had hoped, but after a recce we found that the south side of Rhumsiki Tower, the tallest and highest of the sentinels, offered a decent-looking line. The downside was that all the cracks on the route were filled with dirt and vulture guano. While it would have been possible to climb the route from the ground up in a traditional style, it would have meant an incredibly hard, dirty, dangerous aid climb. We all decided then and there that we had come for fun, so we opted for a top-down approach, so that we could clean out the cracks and secure fixed protection in the form of expansion bolts where necessary before climbing the route.

Later that afternoon, as the towers cast long shadows that crept across the undulating valleys, we stood on top of the spire. One of the Technicals had shown us an easy scramble up the back that they often used for vulture-egg hunting. A hot wind blew in our faces and the vultures circled on thermals. It truly was a fine place to be, deep in the heart of Africa. Below our feet the south face of the spire dropped clear for 300 metres. Ed found some anchors and we threw our ropes over the edge, rappelling down the cliff to prepare our route. It took four days of absolutely filthy work as we unearthed literally tons of guano to regain solid ledges and clear the choked cracks. We used crude sickles purchased from the village for the job, and emerged from a day's work looking like coal miners with faces streaked with sweat and dirt. The vultures watched our every move, and we made certain we stayed well clear of their nests because they had a nasty habit of dive-bombing us if we got too close.

At dawn each day, 20 or more barefoot and scruffily dressed Technicals would be waiting to carry our packs down the hill to the base of the cliff. Fights would erupt as to whom was going to porter our bags, and once the dust had settled, with the winners proudly carrying our backpacks, the entire group would accompany us to the crag. Here they would spend the day sitting at the base strumming home-made tin-and-string guitars, jabbering noisily, and watching us strange foreigners climbing the mighty rock face. In the evening, the process would be reversed and back up at camp, they would watch the evening's proceedings, squatting just outside the pool of light cast by our fire. One quiet lad, who must have been about 12 years old and who wore the same red T-shirt the entire duration of our visit, took a shine to Robin, asking endless questions: Where we lived, what it was like there, what was this and that for, on and on. Sometime during the evening we would hear a shout from the village and the Technicals would melt away home into the darkness while we continued on with a fair amount of imbibing and good-natured ribaldry around the fire. Luckily Cameroon Airlines hadn't lost our whisky.

"So, Ed, how did you spend your holiday?"

"Gardening in Cameroon."

"I thought botanists liked gardening."

"Fuck off."

The nights were cold without a sleeping bag under my rough blanket, and the soles of my sand shoes had delaminated, but things were working out with the gear shortage. I borrowed Simon's harness, used Robin's khaki trekking pants, and Greg and I traded rock shoes, three sizes too big for me, by taking turns on the rock and lowering the shoes afterwards down on the rope. Finally we started climbing, and over the course of a week we ended up doing the route at least twice, as each pitch was carefully filmed by Greg dangling from a rope nearby.

Wherever in the world I climb, the actual climbing is very similar; I could be anywhere because I'm concentrating on the next handhold above me or the next tiny foothold somewhere below. It's only when I leaned back on the anchors, turned around and looked out at the fascinating, desolate scenery of Northern Cameroon that it sank in. This was deepest Africa. I felt it as the hot sun cooked my neck while I climbed the ropes, and when I heard the deep drumbeats vibrating through the valleys and the thick night. It's a continent unlike any other: timeless, elemental and always powerful.

Some of the pitches were fun to climb, others weren't. Ed had chosen to lead the first third of the route, I would do the middle, and Mark the top. Ed's nemesis turned out to be a horrible, wide crack that we endearingly named "The Fissure February" in honour of his struggle to climb it. Too wide to jam his hands into, but too narrow for his body, it was like watching a gorilla trying to do ballet. He shuffled strenuously upwards with half an arm and half a leg jammed into the slot. At one point Simon was moved to politely ask Ed to tone down his cursing because the film footage was turning out to be unusable. A nasty crack on my section kept reducing my hands to mincemeat as I squeezed them tightly against the sharp, painful rock, and by the time we reached Mark's third of the route it was usually late afternoon and he wilted in the slippery 38-degree heat. We had worked pretty hard to make a decent film for National Geographic, and when all the filming was complete, we removed all the ropes and prepared for a continuous ascent from the ground up with no one except the Technicals watching us.

But first we took a rest day and visited the *Féticheur*, the crab sorcerer in Rhumsiki village. He looked ancient – from the depth of his etched face it looked like he had been alive for 100 years or more, and hadn't washed for at least 50 of those. His skill was to tell the future by divining the way river crabs move pottery shards around in a calabash. Squatting in a dusty courtyard, with Robin translating, he came up with some surprising and intuitive answers. He told me I would have two children, which I do. He told Ed he would live in a small village far from water, which he does – some of the time – in Montagu near Cape Town. He told Greg he would go on a great journey. At the end we asked whether our route would be a success and he replied that we would only achieve what we had set out to do if we sacrificed a chicken to ward off danger. Greg reckoned the old man was just conning us for a free meal, which he probably was, but it didn't matter because it was the ritual that counted. He splattered chicken blood on our feet to keep us safe and sent us on our way.

Dawn opened a cool eye on us as we woke up to start our complete ascent the next day. Ed and I climbed together on one rope, Mark and Greg on the other. We blitzed the route in four hours, and it was a great climbing day out. We were all tired, but we kept it together and climbed the route free without hanging on any of the gear. On my crux section, I ripped my hands in the crack again, but I held on and didn't let go. Blood ran down my arms as I reached the end, and I was very relieved that I would never have to do the pitch again.

Ed led the top section and the route was done.

Afterwards we all sat on the porch of the village bar in true colonial style, drinking beer, eating *croque-monsieurs* (Cameroon's version of the French grilled cheese-and-ham sandwiches) and enjoying a fine view over the valley and Rhumsiki Spire. We decided to call our route The Great Technical Adventure after the kids, because they had watched our every move from the moment we arrived. We had completed an excellent route in fine style on a remote wall and we were very pleased. Most expeditions would have ended there, but there was one last outstanding deed to be done: it had to be BASE jumped.

It would be a difficult jump. The first 50 metres were less than vertical, jutting out slightly into my path, and there was a big ledge to miss on the way down. The exit point was a tiny down-sloping ledge that didn't allow for much of a launch to clear the slab below. The next morning I awoke nervous. New jump sites are always scary, and the remoteness of our situation didn't help, but as my foot left the edge and I saw in freefall that I would clear the protruding rock I relaxed. I threw my pilot chute to the wind and the canopy opened and I had a beautiful flight down into the valley below. As I landed, a wave of Technicals came running across the fields towards me. "*Monsieur, vous êtes incroyable!*" (Sir, you are incredible.) I repeated the jump the following morning for the cameras and the two jumps completed the circle of our exploration of the Tower. It was a great privilege to jump off a faraway spire after making the first, and only, ascent of it. I felt content.

It had been a great trip. We'd laughed a lot, drunk a lot on National Geographic's expense account and swapped many legendary stories. We'd lived in the filth and the flies with the Technicals, and Ed had even eaten a beetle one evening, made a loud wish that he could be on expeditions like this for the rest of his life, and then promptly fell into the camp fire. We swiftly rescued him from harm and sat him back up, and handed him another whisky. It was fun and that is what adventure is all about, doing it with friends. You dream up an idea, or see it in a movie, and then you make it happen. But just as you reach one goal, so the others move along in line. There really is no limit to adventure even in this crowded world.

It was just after dawn when we left Rhumsiki and its towers behind. They stood inimitable in their stony, unsettling silence. The Technicals ran after the Jeep for a long time, until they could no longer keep up and then they waved goodbye in a cloud of dust. Time closed behind us and Africa broke into another day.

Well after midnight, some days later, Ed and I sat in the Cameroon Airlines jet in Harare after yet another interminable unscheduled stop. We had long since missed our connecting flights from Johannesburg back to Cape Town, and both of us were looking forward to getting back home to where the concept of time wasn't so relative and where, if you caught a plane, it actually took you where you wanted to go. I turned to Ed and said: "You know, I think I'm getting just a little bit tired of Cameroon Airlines."

Majesty of Silence, casting
Shadows as long as life.
The mountain speaks in dimensions
I cannot hear.
I try to feel the power
Behind the wind and snow,
To know how the emptiness
Can pervade.
It is enough to feel that presence
Amongst these walls of ice,
In the sunset, catching pink,
The highest peaks of silence.

ALPINISM, VOL II

An Instant of Joy

I took a deep breath as I passed the small bronze plaques bolted to the wall. Memorials to climbers killed on the mountain, they were discreetly placed just above the bergschrund, the cleft running between the ice of the glacier and the rocky mountainside. Dawn had broken into a thin slit of red on the horizon, casting enough shadowy light to look up at the 1300 metres of shattered limestone that hung ominously above me. The enormity of what I was about to do flickered briefly to the edge of panic, but I quickly shut it away and turned to look just ahead as I picked out the route through the first rockbands.

"One step at a time, buddy," I told myself. "This is it. Here we go."

It had taken six long years to get to this stage, to where I was about to complete the challenge that I had set myself. But I am a patient man and in the end it didn't seem like a very long time at all. My challenge was to solo the three classic North Faces of the Alps: the Eiger in

Switzerland, the Matterhorn on the Swiss and Italian borders, and the Grandes Jorasses, which is part of the Mont Blanc massif in France, all towering, inspiring and intimidating objects of every alpine climber's desire. I'd actually climbed all of them, at various times with various partners over two very intense alpine summers. And maybe that should have been enough. Why go back and solo them? The easy answer would be "to see if I could do it", but nothing is ever obvious when it comes to the complexity of our drives and motivations.

There is a subtle paradox in soloing. You may feel you are doing it for yourself only, but there could be elements of doing it for yourself as reflected in the admiration of others. Soloing encompasses an intimacy, a sublime beauty in fluid movement, and an intense self-reliance, all of which are counterbalanced sharply by the very real possibility of your own death. So my question cuts directly to the core of why I climb. After many attempts and many years trying to complete this goal, my answer, finally, would be "Because I had to". Simple. Part of the beauty of mountaineering is that we set ourselves challenges we are not sure we can meet. In spite of ourselves, and against all odds, we go out into wild places and try anyway. It's about the human quest, adventure, setting out and not knowing the outcome. Now I had just thrown my fortune to the mist a little higher on the Eiger, and I had to follow it.

Two years previously I had summitted the Grandes Jorasses at dawn via the Walker Spur. I'd climbed the entire route at night by headlight, partly to avoid the crowds but mostly to avoid rockfalls from climbers higher up. On the summit, I watched Monte Rosa glow pink for a minute as the sun rose, and looked down at the Shroud and the Petites Jorasses, picking out the line of Anouk, a route we had done a few days before.

A month later I was on the top of the Matterhorn. I had got there via the Schmidt route, a long ice route which I did in ideal, cold conditions. The ice was thick and I wound my way up, avoiding rock to reach the top and see its large iron cross glinting in the pale sunlight. It was erected as a memorial to four members of the first ascent party who had fallen to their deaths on the way down. Edward

Whymper, an English explorer and one of the three survivors, wrote about the tragedy in his 1871 book, *Scrambles Amongst the Alps*. Here he penned his famous warning to all aspirant mountaineers: "Climb if you will, but remember that courage and strength are naught without prudence, and that a momentary negligence may destroy the happiness of a lifetime. Do nothing in haste; look well to each step; and from the beginning think what may be the end."

As I appeared on the Matterhorn's summit I drew perplexed stares from the Swiss mountain guides short-roping their clients down the Hornli ridge. Bored with guiding the same route over and over, but tremendously proprietorial of what they considered "their" mountain, I could see their minds working hard to place me because they hadn't seen me on their way up and they didn't know from where I had come.

All that was left was the Eiger. I didn't know it at the time, but it was not going to be as easy.

Rising out of grassy meadows high above Alpiglen in the Swiss Alps, the great black amphitheatre of the Eiger is the biggest mountain wall in all of Europe. The North Face, or Nordwand, as it's named in German, has a well-earned reputation for being a challenge. The concave bowl of the Nordwand is prone to savage storms that turn the face into a lethal bowling alley of avalanches, waterfalls and falling rocks. It was first climbed in 1938 by a German-Austrian team after more than a decade of attempts and much nationalistic rivalry. Since 1935 more than 50 climbers have died on the North Face, earning it the nickname Mordwand or "Murder Face". Today it still remains challenging, but that's more due to severe rock falls and shrinking ice fields than to the technical difficulties. In July 2006 the East Face started shedding rock, a precursor to a spectacular rock fall when two-million cubic metres of rock sheered away.

The Eiger is more than just a huge wall. It has a psychological edge, a reputation for trauma and mishap. In his seminal book, *The White Spider*, the German first ascentionist and author of *Seven Years in Tibet*, Heinrich Harrer, delves into the history of the mountain's lore and dark mystique. It's a harrowing read, detailing bold climbers frozen immobile or shattered by rock and recounting horrific tales of misery and suffering. I first read *The White Spider* when I was 12 years old and it transported me to a different world. I knew then that I would climb the Eiger one day. Nine years later I first climbed it with my friend, English climber Sandy Britain. On our ascent I struggled to free the climbing from the aura, battling demons in my head when actually I should have seen it as just another route like any other in Chamonix.

This was my third solo attempt as I climbed towards a feature called the Shattered Pillar over loose, rubbly limestone. I warmed up slowly and found a rhythm, passing a steep gash called the Difficult Crack and moving quickly up easy terrain under the vast rock buttress, the Rote Fluh, to reach the Hinterstoisser Traverse. It is a 30-metre traverse on smooth, blank rock with the wall falling away dramatically beneath your feet as it towers over you, a perilous passage with tiny footholds on the glass-smooth slab. The gateway connecting the lower face to the central section, this has been the scene of several ghastly epics. In 1936, a German party consisting of Andreas Hinterstoisser, a talented young climber and namesake of the traverse, and his three companions came to horrific grief here. Having made a daring traverse that opened up the route to the summit, a storm blew in, forcing them into retreat. But by then the traverse had iced up and as they had withdrawn their rope they were unable to get back across it. Trapped there, they died one by one, either by freezing or by being swept away by rockfalls. Since then climbers have always left a fixed rope behind in case they need to retreat.

As I looked at it, it still looked impregnable: a shield of slabby rock angled at about 70 degrees. It would have been a delicate piece of climbing at the local crag on a sunny day in rock shoes, never mind a third of the way up a menacing wall in mountain boots, with treacherous snow clinging to all the ledges and footholds. But I felt completely detached and emotionless. Now I gave no regard to its history and what had gone before. To climb the route I'd had to become an iceman, distancing myself from it in order to concentrate. Feelings would only come later. The rock was dry and a faded fixed rope was strung across the traverse. I took a deep breath, gathered my mettle, and traversed across it on tiptoes, holding the rope for balance, and soon I was onto easy snow leading up to the Swallows Nest. The sky was cobalt blue beyond the shadow of the wall. I was doing well: it was 10am and I was ahead of my planned schedule.

Seven hours earlier I had lain in the dark meadow far below listening to the distant sound of cowbells. Sleep hadn't come at all, just the endless stream of doubts and fears that arrived like familiar but unwanted guests. I replayed the route continually in my mind, imagining myself on the immense black-and-white wall that blocked out half the clear night sky above me. I have always found visualisation easy. I am able to remember long, complicated sequences on sport routes, clearly imagining how I would grasp a hold or how the change in balance would feel as I weight a tiny foothold. Now, as I imagined the route above me, I had one of those deep senses that everything would be OK. Underneath the tension in my body I simply knew I could do it this time.

I've always had an uncanny sense of intuition when it comes to danger. Three times I have ignored warnings and three times I have been hurt: twice BASE jumping and once when my knee was hit by a falling rock the first time I tried to solo the Walker Spur on the Grandes Jorasses. I strongly believe that we are able to sense the future, not as a soothsayer or fortune teller, but in a subtle no less profound way that underlies our efforts in extreme places. Perhaps it's because we willingly put ourselves into uncertainty that we become more receptive to our intuitions and I credit my staying alive to this. I've abandoned routes, as have my partners turned me away from routes, in perfectly good weather for no reason other than a vague ill feeling. The bottom line is that you have to trust yourself and your instinct. Even then, a large measure comes down to luck. I think of a close call that I had in the Bonatti couloir on the Dru during my second season in the Alps when I came close to being killed by a rockfall. I looked up and the sky was black. My last thought was "Oh fuck!" as the boulders rained around me, missing me by centimetres. To this day I am still amazed at how a couloir full of rocks managed to miss me. There have been other close calls too, on Mont Blanc's Brenva Face and Grand Pilier d'Angle and on the Courtes. Near misses that can only be put down to luck, or fate, or chance, as you roll the dice and gamble with your life. Ernest Hemingway once wrote that there are only two sports, bull-fighting and mountain climbing. All the rest were games. Alpinism is dangerous. But we knew that.

Above the Swallows Nest the first ice field was easy and I made rapid progress up to a feature called the Ice Hose. It was covered with black ice and it looked treacherous. I took the single rope out of my pack, clipped into some rusty pegs, and gave myself some psychological protection as I delicately climbed up using the tips of my crampons on the smooth slab covered by a thin veil of ice. My concentration was intense because a fall would have been disastrous. I was relieved when I reached the top. One crux was safely over.

I moved quickly up and across the 500 metres of the second ice field. The snow was hard and my crampons bit easily and solidly. The wall was in excellent condition: dry rock, firm snow, cold tempera-tures and few falling rocks. I was glad to be there, glad to have waited for this, and exhilarated by the climbing as I relaxed into the move-ment. The rock band at the end, a feature named the Flat Iron after it's distinctive triangular shape, was delicate and surprisingly hard. I balanced crampon points on rock and climbed carefully and with precision, until I reached the Death Bivouac, which owes its macabre name to the two Germans, Karl Mehringer and Max Sedlmeyer, who froze to death here in 1935. I stopped for a rest and a cigarette. I took my pack off, sat down on the ledge, which was about the size of a single bed, and looked down. The wall really was colossal. Below me hundreds of metres of steep ice, snow and black rock fell away into the shadow that stretched far down the green slopes into the sunlight.

It was a wild place to be sitting. My first solo attempt had ended here. I'd started out with Julie and John Stratham, a straight-up young Yorkshireman whom we had befriended in Chamonix. The two of them teamed up as a roped pair while I went ahead alone. Although the forecast was ambiguous we thought we had a good chance, but as I crossed the second ice field rocks bombed down with terrifying high-pitched whines, thudding into the snow. I raced through the rain to reach Death Bivouac, the halfway point on the wall, getting there just in time as the rain changed to snow and the storm hit with a vengeance. Safely sheltered but also helplessly trapped, I huddled in my bivvy bag. As sleet raged beyond and washed the whole wall white, I dozed in a netherworld of isolation, waking startled at 11pm to the incongruous sound of a shout from below. I'd assumed that Julie and John had retreated since they had been so far behind, but two headlamps appeared out of the snowy gloom. They were frozen incomprehensible and hypothermic. I brewed them tea, thawed them out and the three of us lay there, uncomfortably wedged together, for another day and night as the storm slowly spent itself. In my head I planned with cool precision how we would descend the sheer face of that long and unforgiving wall, visualising every single rappel anchor on the route down. And I executed that plan exactly on the third day as cold spindrift blew across the wall. The Eiger no longer held demons for me: I knew I could get off it.

My second solo attempt had ended at the sluice door above the Ice Hose, nearly half way up the Eigerwand. The weather had been on my side, but there was verglas everywhere, treacherous black ice that is slick, slippery and dangerous. The climbing was slow, precarious and extremely nerve-wracking. Without realising that I'd made a conscious decision to bail out, I found myself veering off the route towards a heavy wooden trapdoor that leads into the train tunnel of the Jungfraubahn railway. Amazingly, a cog railway line runs through the middle of the Eiger to the Jungfraujoch, a restaurant and panoramic viewpoint high up on a col between the neighbouring peaks, the Jungfrau and the Munch. The trapdoor had been used by the Swiss railway engineers as a rubble discharge during construction in the 1920s and it is always kept unlocked. It was the right choice. I stepped off the North Wall and into the inky depths of the mountain, which was pitch dark and claustrophobic. I turned on my headlamp immediately because I have never liked caves. There are legends about climbers caught inside this tunnel when a train passes. Lore has it that the trick is to flatten yourself against the rock, breathe out, and turn your head sideways or the train clips you as it chugs slowly upwards. But I was lucky and no trains ran while I was inside.

Thirty minutes later I walked out of the tunnel, blinking in the sharp sunlight above Kleine Scheidegg, the railway station and hotel at the foot of the mountain. It had been a strange day on a strange mountain but I'd known, even before I began, that I was destined to fail. The Canadian lyricist and singer, Margo Timmins, once made an interesting observation about life. She said: "You can always see it coming, but you can never stop it." I had to try, until the senselessness of continuing became apparent. There is such a fine balance between ambition and judgement that it is often difficult to separate the two, but I think that if you listen carefully and are honest with yourself, the clear choice is always evident.

I finished my cigarette, drank some of the litre of water I was carrying, and ate some chocolate. I was focused and ready. I stepped onto the third ice field, which had been pockmarked by falling rocks but was still frozen hard, and climbed across into the Ramp and up the icy chimneys in the back of this narrow passage which cleaves two blank rock walls. I was feeling strong when I reached the Waterfall pitch, the crux of the upper wall. Just as well, it looked tricky. Globs of ice and needle-like chandeliers were draped over a small overhang at the top of the chimney like a bizarre, lopsided ice-cream cone that had melted and then refrozen. It would have to be chopped away to give me access to the higher reaches above it. I was apprehensive but calm as I pulled out the rope again to protect myself, and precariously balanced my crampon points on rock footholds as I tiptoed up. At the ice-cream cone, I hung with one hand wedged into a crack while with the other I carefully and very methodically demolished all the ice hanging over the lip of the overhang. Chopping it away with my axe until it was all gone, I made myself a decent passage through it. Then I ever so cautiously tiptoed my feet higher until I could dig both ice picks in over the lip and climb over the overhang. I'm a careful solo climber, preferring never to take chances or get myself into precarious situations, and the whole way up I climbed very deliberately. Over the bulge I slowly climbed up a steep ice-filled chimney and onto a hanging snowfield above, always very much in control.

I suddenly became aware that there was sunlight on the buttress above me. My concentration had been so intense I'd seen nothing but the ice before me. The Eiger catches the sun in the afternoon near the Traverse of the Gods and as I climbed diagonally past loose rock on the Brittle Ledges and into the traverse, I felt as if the gods were smiling at me. Everything had clicked into place. The White Spider, so named because the snow-filled cracks clinging to the rock surrounding the snowfield resemble the legs of a spider, was solid ice and I made rapid progress up to the Exit Cracks. It was a wild place to be: high above the ground with blue-grey hazy verticality dropping straight down to the meadows below. There was nowhere else I would rather have been.

The White Spider narrows at the top into the Exit Cracks, a labyrinthine web of gullies. When Sandy Britain and I had been there previously we'd spent half a day struggling up the wrong one in a storm and blinding snowfall. This time the correct gully was easy to recognise and I could see the final obstacle, a feature named the Quartz Crack near the top where the snow gully pinched in before opening out onto the upper snowfields. I was close now and keen to keep going but I made myself stop at the top of The White Spider to eat nougat, drink water, and smoke a cigarette. I calmed down with Edward Whymper's century-old refrain hanging unspoken in the afternoon air: "Do nothing in haste, and look well to each step."

I felt a brief prerecognition of success, a tiny voice inside me said, "Yes, you've done it", but it was only a momentary lapse of concentration that I quickly squashed, because nothing is ever finished until it's done, until you're safely down.

I focused my concentration again as I climbed up easy mixed runnels. A final roped belay on awkward climbing in the Quartz Crack, and the way above was clear. The white, easy-angled snowfield went straight to the top. I sunk my axes into the snow like walking sticks and carefully kicked steps upwards with my boots. The snow was soft and it stuck to my crampons, making them slippery and ineffective as the balled-up snow flattened out the spikes. Every second or third step I had to whack the shaft of my axe against my boots to clear the snow off them, because this was no place to slip. I suddenly became painfully conscious of the yawning void that stretched 2000 metres below me. I felt very exposed after the narrow confines of the wall and with utmost care I made sure that each foot placement was good and solid before kicking the next step. The Eiger refused to release its grip on me until the very end.

Fifteen hours after crossing the bergschrund, I stepped over the northeast ridge. The route was done. It was 7pm and not much daylight remained. I had no time to linger in the thinning light as I had to get as far down the West Ridge as I could before darkness fell. A glance from the summit was all I had time for. And all I needed. Below me, long shadows crisscrossed a beautiful and desolate world, punctuated by the sharp, pale yellow peaks of the Dent Blanche, Arolla, Midi, and Mont Blanc glowing far to the west in the evening sun. It was just an instant, but it contained so much: familiarity, strangeness and ultimately sadness. In that transient other world, I was a stranger and yet I belonged. I had risked everything to get there, only to discover that there had been nothing there for me in the first place. It was like I had been trying to catch a cloud with my hands. I suppose I had been looking for something more, but there really is nothing to find on the summit of a mountain other than yourself.

I headed down as fast as I dared, winding my way over loose rubble. I followed indistinct cairns that marked the way, dropping down steep cliffs and slick ice fields, peering harder and harder into the gloom as the light ebbed. After dark I slowed down, winding left and right and all over, trying to pick out the easiest way down in the narrow pool of torch light in a jet-black night, and always unsure if I was on the right route. I had finished my water some time ago and I was thirsty, but I still felt strong and I knew nothing would stop me until I got down. I picked my way down over steep rocks and scree. A short rappel over a cliff that I couldn't seem to bypass put me onto what I thought was the last snowfield, and gradually the angle eased. Suddenly I spotted the railway tracks glinting in my headlamp beam. It was all over. With a mental sigh I relaxed the iron grip of concentration that had locked my head in vice-like focus. Finally I could ease up, because I was safe and alive and very, very tired. I cut above Kleine Scheidegg across the meadows to my gear, numbly made a cup of tea and fell asleep, completely drained.

Morning came softly. It was to be another bluebird day. Overnight, my body had drunk in the sleep it so badly needed and the powerful intensity of the previous day had melted away. I woke up feeling very much alive. I packed and wandered over to a couple of tents in the next meadow where two Italian girls were watching their friends on the lower wall through binoculars. I took a turn and spotted them under the Rote Fluh. I automatically started to trace the route upwards and then I stopped and lowered the binoculars so that I could barely make out the two climbers. I'd seen enough. It was only then that the true scale of what I'd done sank in. The wall looked absolutely immense, a colossus. It seemed impossible that only a few hours previously I had been up there.

To achieve what I had, I had mentally broken down the whole route into manageable chunks that I could get my head around comfortably, and now that it was over the whole overwhelmed me. I was exhilarated, electrified. I had finished something that I had set out to do alone. I wished the Italians good luck and strode down to Grindelwald, my senses alive, the vibrancy of colour, sound and smell bringing magic to the Swiss pastoral scenery around me.

Eventually, and inevitably, the excitement turned to fulfilment which then drained into a deep melancholy, but that's always the case when you have given your all towards a goal you've finally reached. A few weeks later, as I watched the rain pouring down from beneath sheltered eaves overlooking a deserted Rue Paccard, the main street in Chamonix, I realised that I had finally finished with the Alps. Its peaks had dominated my life for six years, but I had served my apprenticeship and now I was ready to move on to bigger things. The Eiger had been my swansong in a way.

But what I didn't recognise as I drove out of Chamonix on the long road to Paris, and eventually to home, was that above and beyond all the years of climbing, it was my brief instant on the summit of the Eiger that carried a lifetime's worth of joy.

There is a solitude of space
A solitude of sea
A solitude of death, but those
Society shall be
Compared with that profounder site
That polar privacy
A soul admitted to itself –
Finite infinity

EMILY DICKINSON, 1830–1886

Fathers

After you'd gone I sat on your bed and almost cried. The last time I'd seen you, you'd lain there clinging to life with all you had and not letting go. Just like you had taught me never to let go. Your bed was empty, but even when you had lain in it, there wasn't much of you left. All that remained of a lifetime was some musty, old man's clothing, photographs of us – your children and some mildewed letters. It was hard not to cry but I didn't and somehow I couldn't. I don't know why.

The empty room was bright and sunlight poured through the window, so different to the last time we were together when black anvils of angry thunderclouds marched across the evening summer sky, intent on furious vengeance. It had rained, a rain that had sluiced and gushed across the parched earth around us. My words that evening became a torrent too as they poured from me. I think you must have heard me, I hope so, but I don't know if you did. It doesn't really matter because I needed to say those things anyway. But if you did hear me on that black, sweet-smelling rain-soaked evening what I said was quite simple: thanks for being my father.

I looked up to you. You were my hero once. You seemed so strong and you knew everything. And then you were gone. I was 12 years old when you left home and life carried on without you. Strangely enough, I didn't really miss you at the time. That only came later when it was too late. Our lives diverged and with every passing day there was less and less we had in common. Except that blood is stronger than that, and I should have realised how much you missed us, your children scattered across the globe like the dandelions that we'd blown into the wind all those years ago. And yet when I returned to South Africa, we still did not connect. Perhaps some of that has to do with the shame I felt about you finding solace in the bottom third of your whisky bottle, but perhaps not. Our lives moved on, mine into middle age, yours into old age, but I always thought of you as my gentle and omnipresent father, someone who was always there.

I never really understood why it all unravelled for you and I don't think you could have told me. When I brought my son, your grandson, to see you for the first time I could see that you were affected, but I will never know how much. That is my loss and your loss too: to miss out on that enduring and powerful connection that is family.

One of the best memories I have of you is when we went hiking in the Drakensberg, just the two of us, you and me. I was nine years old. We walked up the Tugela Gorge and camped at Tugela Cave at Mont-aux-Sources. We ate Toppers and Smash, disgusting dehydrated mincemeat and mashed potatoes, but to me it was a king's banquet. I was passionate about the mountains even then and you, in your own small way, helped to start me on the long path I was to follow years later. I'm grateful for that weekend we spent together and I'll always cherish those memories. I told you all this during that rain-soaked night and maybe you heard me, but maybe you didn't. You can spend a lifetime with someone and still only remember a few fleeting moments, because those are the only ones that really matter.

Just before you died Ed came to see me all agitated with something to say. Eventually he said it: go to your father, he needs you and you need him. You see, after you left Ed stepped into your shoes. He became my surrogate father, mentor, confidante and friend. It's a different kind of relationship, but he stepped into the empty place that you had left behind like a fleeting shadow. He became the man I looked up to and aspired to be. His was the calm guiding voice saying finish your degree, you can always climb afterwards, and he was the one who held my rope in the early years when I ventured into the blinding, meandering passion that is climbing.

I want to do it differently this time. I want to continue what you started but were not quite able to finish. I want my children to grow up secure and happy and content, to know that their father will always come home to them. I want to be the father who will be there, the father I know you really wanted to be. I want to play with them in the warm sea just as we used to. I want them to ride on my back as the waves crash over us, just as I hung onto your back for dear life. And I want to laugh with them and watch them grow up and not miss out on a thing. I want to keep the continuity going and I want to be the plug in the yawning gap of sorrow that somehow opened between me and you. Goodbye, Dad. I miss you.

Rodney the Heap

Ed and I seem to have an uncanny knack of finding ourselves in the middle of a minor epic without realising it. The blizzard had finally become so bad that we couldn't continue any further: snowdrifts piled high around us and thick, heavy snow braided everything into a white crystal sheet. Night was fast approaching, and it looked like a bivouac would be inevitable. Ed peered into the gloom as the cold crept in around us and said dryly, "Hmm, I feel a nip in the air, reminds me of Pearl Harbour."

We weren't on Everest or the Alps, nor were we anywhere remotely close to mountains. Instead, we sat inside a car half-covered in snow in the middle of the M1 motorway somewhere in the flat farmlands of Sussex, 100 miles (160 kilometres) from London. Unbeknownst to us, we were travelling in the United Kingdom in the middle of the worst winter storm in half a century. Oak trees that had stood firm for 500 years lay uprooted on the side of the highway. But how were we to know anything was amiss when this was our first visit to the British Isles? For all we knew this was normal winter weather. We also didn't know we'd spend that first night in England in jail.

Ed was curled up on the front seat in his sleeping bag with a steaming cup of tea when a gloved hand wiped drifted snow from the window and a voice said: "Sorry, sirs, you can't stay here, you'll have to come with me." Ed rolled down the window a crack to reveal the looming spectre of a policeman, to whom he offered, with an air of bonhomie, a cup of tea. The policeman politely declined. We were well equipped for camping in the car, even if we were in the middle of a highway. We had food, a stove, sleeping bags, winter climbing gear and plenty of books. We were quite happy to remain where we were, but the policeman was adamant. Not long afterwards our car, Rodney the Heap, was pulled out of the snowdrift by an army Land Rover and towed to the side of the road. Then we were driven in the same Land Rover to a small village, I forget the name, where we spent the night in the police station cells with a salesman, a prostitute and a thief, none of whom were on their way to Llanberis Pass in North Wales to climb Cenotaph Corner or the Left Wall. The thief explained that he made a living stealing bicycles and then selling them in Amsterdam, the prostitute clearly needed her next heroin fix and the salesman looked very uneasy. The policemen fed us jail food on plastic plates with little compartments separating the chicken and vegetables. It was quite tasty, actually. Prison graffiti made interesting bedtime reading, although it was mostly names and dirty jokes that were scratched into the cinder block walls. Ed and I shared a cell – with an open door – and we slept soundly on the hard bunks. In the morning all of us, I'm sure, were only too happy to leave.

Two days later we dug Rodney out of yet another drift on the side of the motorway, to reveal him in all his frost encrusted glory. Some months previously, Ed and I had found the car in France with the help of Didier Trousseau, a French friend of ours. It was a Citroën 2CV Deux Chevaux (Two Horses), which cost 600 Francs, which was quite cheap even back then. Today it probably converts to about R3000. From a distance Rodney had looked in pretty good shape, but on closer inspection he turned out to be a complete wreck. Powered by a two-cylinder engine, not much more than glorified a lawnmower engine really, he was a rattling old contraption held together with some bits of wire and not too much else. But he had four wheels and he could drive, after a fashion, with a sound that was not unlike a bed sheet being torn in half. And we were psyched because we had become mobile and could go climbing. Ed named the car "Rodney" after his beer-loving brother, because it tended to drink a lot of oil and, in spite of itself, still had plenty of stamina. We loaded our gear into the back and were constantly surprised at how much stamina Rodney had, as he carried us, gears whining and pistons screaming, over tortuous alpine roads.

Rodney was a magnet for cops. We would be driving peacefully down the road, well below the speed limit, on our way to the crag when I would happen to glance in the one remaining rear-view mirror (on the passenger side) and see flashing lights. *Gendarmerie*, Police, *Carabinieri* or *Polizei*, they were all the same. "Here we go again," Ed or I would sigh. They always hauled us out, checked our papers, examined the car and then let us go with a warning to do this, or that, or the next thing, which we never did. Like fix the roof because there was a gaping hole in it where a friend had put a rope heavy with ice through the vinyl in the Vallée de La Romanche in France, after we had climbed a frozen waterfall in brittle temperatures of minus 40 degrees Celsius.

We were stopped by the cops in virtually every country in Europe, and I guess I can't blame them after all the numerous mechanical mishaps and misadventures we'd had, each one making Rodney look even more of a wreck than the last. Somebody drilled a bolt hanger onto the back for convenient belaying. The exhaust was held together with a Coke can and wire. We came within an inch of taking out a red Maserati in Monte Carlo, after an Australian climber that we had given a lift to, left the handbrake off. The bonnet blew off going down the highway one day because I had neglected to tie it back on after an oil stop, and a small collision on a one lane road in the Cairngorms in the eastern Scottish Highlands had thrown the whole frame out of line. Rodney limped like a dog with a broken leg, crabbing his way down the road and scrubbing all the tyres bare.

About nine months after the wheel alignment accident Chris Lomax, a fellow South African climber, and I were driving through the flat industrial heartland of northern France en route to Chamonix one blisteringly hot Sunday afternoon, when one of the long suffering tyres finally had a blow-out. We put on the spare, which was only marginally better, and drove less than a kilometre down the road before we were pulled over by a gendarme, yet again. He inspected the tyre we had just changed and was horrified at how bald it was, and then – I knew it was coming – he demanded to see our "spare", which was lying in shreds in the boot. There followed the predicted Gallic horror. His eyes rolled back as he said things like "*Oh la la*" and "*Merde!*". Ordering us to follow him to the nearest village, he made us buy four brand-new Michelin tyres. He also made the mechanic heat up the rear axle and pound it back into line. Then he bade us "*Bon voyage et bonne escalade*" with a ticket for disturbing him on what should otherwise have been a quiet Sunday afternoon beat. In one afternoon I had used up half the money I had saved for the entire summer, but I didn't care because a whole season of alpine climbing lay ahead. That summer I ended up doing a lot of walking to save on *telepherique* (cable-car) fares. And I had a lucky break when the teller at a Bureaux de Change added two zeros to a traveller's check by mistake, which meant I could keep climbing instead of picking grapes or washing beer glasses at the Bar Nationale.

Over time Rodney developed a stubborn fickleness in his ability to start. Ed had taken most of the ignition to pieces and still couldn't get it to work, so we learned to park on hills and became experts at spotting the most likely motorists to have jumper cables to get us started again. Outside Avignon one morning, Moose, Julie and I were caught red-handed "sport farming". We were stealing a box of ripe apples from an orchard when the farmer spotted us and came running, yelling and brandishing a spade. It was like a classic scene from a B-grade movie, except that Rodney, our trusty getaway car, refused to start at the critical moment. Which lead to a rather awkward situation, with plenty of insults spat on us filthy English foreigners. But luckily for us the Tour de France had just come to a nail-biting finish, with American Greg LeMond battling Belgian cycling legend Eddie Merckx for first place over the line. The American won, and as soon as the farmer discovered that Julie was American everything changed and we became instant friends. Julie ended up baking him a delicious apple pie in his kitchen on a giant cast-iron stove, and we drove away with an even bigger box of apples that he had given us, along with a jumpstart from his tractor.

Rodney had another slightly more serious bug and that was his appetite for steering wheels. We were driving into the campsite at Apt after a day's climbing at Buoux when the steering wheel suddenly came away in my hands. The knuckle joint at the end of the steering wheel shaft had broken off. Luckily for us, almost every village in France has a junkyard on the outskirts if you look carefully enough, and invariably there were one or two old 2CVs from which we could scavenge spare steering wheels. Rodney went through a steering wheel a week on average, but for the long drive back to the UK from southern France we had planned ahead and managed to wedge five spare steering wheels next to the two Kiwi climbers who hitched a ride with us. Border crossings in Rodney tended to be rather lengthy affairs at the best of times, but that crossing at Dover topped them all. Simon Middlemass, one of the New Zealanders, even managed to take a nap during the four hours it took customs to take the car apart and put it back together in their search for drugs we didn't have. We were strip-searched, questioned separately, and then requestioned, and our stories must have corroborated because they finally let us go. We were just honest young climbers after all. As we drove off Simon turned to me and said, "Ya know, I reckon it must have been the steering wheels in the back that tipped them off."

The last time I saw Rodney was when I parked him for the final time down an alley in Wimbledon, a swanky London neighbourhood, stashing him away. A French couple was walking their dog as I did so, and the woman came rushing up to me in excitement to ask if I were French. Her face fell with disappointment when I replied "*Non madame*, I am South African. I am leaving England this evening." They continued their walk down that damp street far from home as I stowed the three remaining steering wheels in the back, locked the door and flew home. Some months later, Andy Wood, another South African friend of ours, needed a car in Europe and I drew him a map of how to find Rodney and handed him the keys. But Rodney apparently drove six blocks and then died forever. Perhaps it was because neither Ed nor I were there to coax some more inspiration into him, or perhaps it was just that he had had enough, but Rodney decided not to cooperate any further. His was a lonely fate on a grey London street, also far from home.

Andy Wood brought back the keys and the registration papers, and I kept them for quite a while, not ready to let go of an old friend. I imagine that poor old Rodney the Heap probably found his end crushed into a rusting piece of compressed metal in some British automotive scrap yard after the police had failed to trace the registered owners who had long gone and moved on to different things. Rodney was the ultimate dream car: he took us to places where our dreams came true. For a year and a half we drove, lived and slept in him, we nursed, cajoled, kicked and swore at him, and still he kept going, whining and rattling and taking us to the bottom of whatever climb we had set our sights on. Those policemen could not have known how much fun we had had with Rodney, nor how much freedom that beaten-up wreck had given a bunch of climbers.

I sometimes wish I could have been there to watch Rodney's final encounter with the police as they towed him away, to watch from a distance, to laugh and to whisper a word of thanks to him for keeping it together for us. Because I doubt the police saw the humour in the three steering wheels stashed in the back.

Milner

It was almost dusk on a hot day in January when Ed and I clambered to the summit of Milner Peak. Evening shadows lay long across the Hex River Mountains, the rugged edges softened in the last golden light. It could have been momentous, a perfect ending to a long and brutal ascent. Below us, in deep shade, dropped the huge, scooped-out East Face we'd just climbed. You might have expected a congratulatory handshake, a triumphant yell, or some other shared communion that comes with a partnership of the rope. But instead Ed turned away and said, "Come on, let's piss off. I've had enough." We turned and plodded down into the gloom, glad to have finished what had become an unyielding nemesis.

Milner is fantastic. Here huge rock walls plunge off towering ridges and disappear into bush-choked kloofs. Valleys and ridges twist and curve like grotesque architecture, free of form and intent. And then, as if by way of a masterstroke, the huge east amphitheatre of Milner Peak caps the labyrinthine landscape: the architect's chuckling signature. The wall rises nearly 400 metres off a steep and rocky talus slope, a scooped and overhanging bowl of alternating bands of shale and red quartzite. It's an impressive cliff in a wild place and it's in our own backyard so, of course, we had to climb it.

The forces of geological compression and upliftment must have been quite something to shape Milner and give it its buckled terrain; indeed, the forces pressed the rock so hard that most of the cracks squeezed shut. The result is a towering, smooth rock wall, like the sheer glass facade of a city skyscraper.

We weren't worried though, because big walls always look blank from a distance. Up close, there are inevitably tiny features and small weaknesses that can be pieced together to form a climbing route. And when we first saw Milner Amphitheatre from a distance it looked perfectly climbable, with lots of features. We had a lot to learn about Milner.

It was all Ed's idea. He had seen the wall while walking in the Hex River Mountains with his brother Rodney as a teenager, and he had always resolved to go back and climb it. Our first attempt 17 years ago ended exactly 10 metres off the ground after I had taken several nine-metre falls. If I'd climbed any higher, I would've hit the ground for sure. We had no bolts and all we could see was inhospitable blank rock as far up as our craned necks allowed, but we were young and keen back then. We thought nothing of the nine hours it took us to thrash our way from the lonely road-head up a dark kloof to the wall, or of the near-ground falls and blank bits of rock face. We resolved to come back.

But life got in the way: we climbed bigger and higher walls in other parts of the world, earned degrees, careers, broken bones and money (and then spent it all on more climbing trips). But in the back of our minds there was always Milner Amphitheatre. Unclimbed. Nothing gnaws at a climber's heart more than unfinished business, so we had to go back. Somebody had to climb it.

In the winter of 1997 Ed recruited Ian Manson, a fellow vagabond South African climber with extensive experience on the colossal granite walls of Yosemite, USA, to help with the arduous task of carrying in a barrel full of equipment in readiness for a future attempt. In early 1998 I arrived back in Cape Town after a decade away in the USA, and Ed and I spent several days carrying in the rest of the gear. This was serious work as we hauled huge quantities of rope and steel through thick bush and up steep slopes to the wall. But finally all was in place. Ed and I stood at the base of the cliff next to a small mountain of gear and gazed upwards. By then Manson was icebound somewhere in Antarctica, after taking on a job as safety coordinator for a group of Japanese scientists. We were fully prepared for a full-aid route. Our plan was to drill a bolt ladder up the first 60 metres of blank shale, and then get into the "natural" aiding, where we would use mechanical devices balanced, wedged or pounded into cracks from which to hang while we placed the next piece a little higher. In this way we would inch our way up the steep and difficult rock.

The moment that you step off the ground into the transition zone between the horizontal world and the vertical is always a little uneasy, even intimidating. But soon concentration takes over and before you know it, you're high off the ground. We'd brought a power drill to aid us through this section: a 24-volt, battery-powered beast called a Bosch Bulldog that we hung off our harnesses as we climbed. It was like being on a construction site as we pressed the drill onto the hard stone, pulled the trigger and the Bulldog ate its way into the rock. Ed and I played a game with it: we'd see how many hook moves we could do before our nerve broke and we'd hurry to drill a bolt for security. A skyhook is a curved piece of steel that you place precariously on a shallow indent of rock or on the lip of a shallow hole and then rest your weight on it. Nerve-racking at best, they are usually downright terrifying to hang on, because the slightest tremor can cause them to pop off and send you plummeting. I reached 15 hook moves in a row before seeing the madness in the game and drilling rivets the rest of the way.

Gravity is a powerful force on Milner. Even at the end of the first pitch, a mere 60 metres up, you feel like you are way off the ground and almost insecure tied into the belay. It's as if the pull of gravity is higher there. The 'Hex' in the Hex River Mountains is perhaps singularly appropriate, because there is a slight air of bewitchment to the place. It's completely intangible, but everyone who has climbed or BASE jumped here has felt it.

Ed started up the second lead into an overhanging corner, and discovered the next surprise Milner had in store for us. Standing precariously on a delicate cam he'd wedged behind a loose flake of rock, he tried to fit a peg into a crack, but no luck. You can hear when the piton has bottomed out: the sound remains constant and you can hammer until your arm falls off but the peg will go no further. The crack was impenetrable, the rock flint-hard and compact and anywhere else we could possibly wedge our gear was loose or rotten. "Send up the drill." Our only recourse was to drill into the rock and place a bolt or a rivet. Beside being slower, it wasn't the way we wanted to climb the route.

After an uncomfortable night on a portaledge – and a hungry one after Ed dropped the food bag – we were back on the rock. We had planned to finish the route in a long weekend. "We'll polish the sucker off for sure!" But our long weekend ended a pitch higher. It seemed as if Milner Amphitheatre was braced against us. What wasn't nerve-jarringly loose was blank rock, impossible to climb. As we rappelled to the ground, I wondered whether we should be there at all. It was as if we were pounding our heads against the wall …

But, of course, a few weeks later we were back, this time with Manson, who was a little wobbly after stepping off the ship from Antarctica that morning. We jumared back up to our high point and carried on up over evermore challenging loose rock, until the three of us found ourselves on a small foot ledge, hanging off our ropes and gazing up at the next imposing section. Bulging, red, overhanging and glass smooth, we'd named this feature The Shield. Ed first looked over to the left at unclimbable shattered, loose grey dihedral, then right at a series of blank corners 100 metres away. Then he looked back up at The Shield, scratched the hair on his beard and said, "Yup, I reckon we should just go straight up."

We drilled our way through The Shield, and in a way it turned out to be one of the best pitches on the route. It was quite a position to be in, hanging off a hook on a 45-degree leaning wall capped by a four-and-a-half-metre horizontal roof. The rock was copper-coloured in the early morning sunlight, and for a time the space below felt friendly instead of menacing. It's simple moments in high wild places like these that make all the effort and labour worth it.

Another complex pitch higher with surprisingly few bolts put us back into good spirits. The rock was improving, there were enough features to get natural gear into and we felt like we were getting somewhere. We reached a sloping ledge and fixed our high point for the following summer when we thought we would return. And then down, down, over the edge we spun, down our long line of fixed rope to the ground.

We didn't know it, but it would be three years before we would be back.

In those three years I'd taken up BASE jumping again and Milner Amphitheatre became the big prize. I returned often, my pack not filled with climbing gear, but with a compact parachute. During the six hours it took to walk up the side to the summit I'd plenty of time to look at the rope we'd fixed. It stopped abruptly two-thirds of the way up the wall. It was like a nagging cold, an unpaid bill, or some other obligation you try to ignore, but can never forget. Our high point gave me a mental ache. I would look away and continue walking. And then I'd leap off the top into that concave bowl of air and it was unfamiliar rock that I saw between my legs as I tracked away in freefall. I would jump, pack and jump again, but no matter how hard I tried to avoid its nagging, our route remained unfinished and incomplete. The mental ache got worse when I thought about going back up there: back to the big struggle with blank rock, the heaving of equipment and the hanging and drilling. Ed and I knew we would have to go back. Something started has to be finished, no matter how difficult it may be. Tenacity was all that remained.

And so in December 2000 we found ourselves back at the base for what we thought would be the final push. It felt different after three years; the sharp edges of the rock seemed like bared fangs snarling at our return. The wall felt oppressive and nasty. We reclimbed the route because our ropes had long since decayed in the sunlight. Bolts seemed further apart, the rock looser, the belays less secure. Perhaps it was our state of mind, but it really felt scary being there, almost as if Milner did not want us. There was no tranquility; we were unwanted guests.

It took us two days to climb to our old high point, and then Ed lead off on what we hoped would be the final aid pitch before easier free-climbing to the summit. Above me he thrashed and cursed his way up complicated blind corners and seams, while I belayed, eating chocolate biscuits in the sun.

Aid climbing is a bipolar affair: you're either on or off. If you're leading you have to control the rising panic and sheer terror of hanging on bits of metal barely holding your body weight. Hours pass like minutes as you engineer a complex line of placements and earn valuable centimetres of height. On the other hand, when you're belaying you're completely out of the loop, half comatose and bored stiff. But then when the lead changes you're on again, and electricity flows from the switch directly into your veins. Terror rises.

Ed belayed at a small ledge perched at the very lip of the last overhang. "How does it look above?" I asked. "Uh, you'll have to come and take a look." Above us were 15 metres of totally blank rock before the angle changed. We had three rivets left, enough to get us a mere three metres off the ledge. Milner had beaten us again. As we rappelled I could have sworn I heard laughter in the echoing silence.

We returned a few weeks later with enough hardware to build the Eiffel Tower, determined not to be stopped short again. But our attitudes had changed. I looked on that last session as just another "attempt". As we walked in my spirit felt light and relaxed, and I remembered an old proverb: "Never do anything to get it over with." Perhaps we had been expecting too much each time we'd been in previously, and maybe that's why we'd underestimated the route so severely. Manson declined to join us this time, but he was an invisible partner in our attempt after all the drudgery that had gone before, as Ed and I regained the little ledge below the blank wall.

And it turned out that 10 little rivets was all it took to bring us up to the easy free-climbing to the top and the walk-off ledge. We had braced ourselves for a final, almighty struggle, which never came. It was like pushing over a monolith with your little finger. We were completely taken by surprise at how easy and anti-climactic the end was. Our nemesis was beaten.

The next morning I walked up to the exit point, a small ledge the size of a single bed jutting out over the top of the wall. As always just before a BASE jump, my senses sharpened acutely as I strapped on my parachute. One of the things I really like about BASE jumping is the extreme personal focus of the event. It's one of the few moments when you are intensely alone. Perhaps it's similar to the approach of your own mortality. But with BASE jumping you get to set your fear and instinct aside and purposefully step off the edge into transformation and renewal. I suppose it's like a modern-day rite of passage, of cleansing, made possible by the technology that allows us to jump off cliffs and survive.

But up there at the exit point I didn't think about any of that. There it was just me and the abyss. Nothing else matters when the moment comes to launch off the edge into another world. Then I committed myself and my fate into my own hands and went.

Beyond the edge is a place of immediacy like no other, especially when you jump into a concave bowl of air like Milner. There are visual references on all sides and below you. It feels like you're jumping into a hole. I swept my arms back into a track and relaxed, enjoying the sensation of accelerating. I was in control, and it felt right. I watched the cliff between my outstretched legs and I looked at the features we had climbed on the way up as I hurtled past. The fourth pitch; the third red overhang; the second red overhang (The Shield) and first red overhang (our three-year high point). I threw the pilot chute into the wind. My canopy opened beautifully and life slowed down as I glided past the steep talus to land on the slope below the wall.

Perhaps that was the full stop that will allow me to move on to other projects without the nagging of an unfinished route, the end of a loop started 18 years before. We'd struggled for so long, but I think that was our problem; we'd always wanted to finish up so that we could move on to other things, other commitments, other plans. Climbing is like a mirror: it's nothing in itself, only a reflection of the effort and energy you put into it. If you struggle against a blank rock wall, you will find struggle to deal with. If you're relaxed and tranquil, the climbing will feel effortless. A mirror doesn't lie. It was a long, hard journey and I'm glad it's over now.

We called our route Mediocrity.

Why "Mediocrity"? When we first started the route, we resolved to leave the bolts at home because we were hoping for a really good, clean route to bisect that unclimbed face.

Through all the nine-metre falls on the first attempt we maintained that noble resolution. Later we realised we were not going to climb the route without some aid: no clean line existed. And we lost heart for about three years. Around this time a good friend, Duncan Elliot, derided us at a party, saying we had reduced the climb to our own level of mediocrity. Maybe.

But maybe "Tenacity" would have been a good name too.

Perhaps the second ascensionists will have an easier time of it.

Fear: (noun) An emotion excited by threatening evil or
impending pain, accompanied by a desire to avoid or
escape it; apprehension; dread.

Courage: (noun) That quality of mind which meets danger
or opposition with intrepidity, calmness, and firmness;
the quality of being fearless; bravery.

OXFORD ENGLISH DICTIONARY

The Opposite of Fear

I've spent a lot of time being afraid. I know the feeling well. I know
exactly how it feels when my tongue sticks to the top of my dry mouth
and I just can't seem to get enough spittle going. I know the sensation
of my chest tightening and the uncomfortable prickling tickle I get
deep inside, just under my ribs. And I know very well the hollow
echo of my heartbeat as it thuds behind my ears. I know what it's like
to be afraid. I also know, intimately, the instinct of wanting to run
away to avoid it.

But in all the years that Fear and I ventured out together I never
had a good look at my companion. I never thought about its nature or
our relationship as I, willingly and with wide-open eyes, put myself
into risky situations time and time again. Fear wove itself into the
substructure of my life until I would not have known myself without
it and yet I never stopped to examine it. I never stopped until I was
forced to stop.

It took my knee-crunching slam into the ground at Milner Peak to
stop me in my tracks, to give me time to think. In the yawning three
months of inactivity, discomfort and crutches that followed I started
thinking about what Fear really is, and what it means to me.

I studied philosophy and psychology at university and I always have
to look at the "why" of things, I can't seem to help myself. I have

A taxing overhanging climb like this keeps me grounded. Air and high rock are my world's of choice, my sanctuaries.

58

59

60

61

Greg and Ed became my instant boyhood heroes when I first saw pictures of their awe-inspiring exploits on the legendary walls of Yosemite.

62

Into the big blue. For a short while we inhabit the world of birds.

OPPOSITE: *Getting pumped on overhanging rock in the Cedarberg. Strength and stamina are vital in your battle against gravity.*

Higher and steeper than I could ever have believed, an expedition to Gasherbrum 4 (left and above) in Pakistan takes an enormous amount of planning, freight management and manpower.

72

73

74

Like ants on the vast slopes of Gasherbrum 4 (above), where altitude robs you of breath, we laid the groundwork for our alpine-style ascent. Myself (top left), Steve Swenson and Steve House (bottom left and right) had as much on our minds as the porters' loads that Gulam Rasool was weighing (centre).

OVERLEAF: *A Namibian sunset at Spitzkoppe. Quiet moments in big places.*

76 ➤

77

78

A Scream in Stone. Cerro Torre's slender spire on a perfect Patagonian day and a tired but elated Julie rappelling down after summitting. Take a good look, such a clear day is a rare gift.

ABOVE: *And here comes the weather as I put my hood up and braced myself for the onslaught on one of our prior attempts.*

80

A machine-gunned row of Cesare Maestri's bolts leads to the top of Cerro Torre.

OVERLEAF: *The point of no return. Jumping from the top of the notorious Ponti building in Johannesburg's Hillbrow badlands. I'm not sure if it's more dangerous inside or outside this building.*

always been much more interested in why people do things than what they have done. What lies beneath is far more important than what we see on the surface. As Plato pointed out in about 400BC, it's much more comfortable to stay in the brightly lit areas of our lives, but that's to deny the whole story. The meaning of the shadows flickering against the walls of the cave of our life is also real. I needed answers beyond the superficial and the experiential. I needed to understand fully why I felt such a pressing need to put myself at risk in the mountains and jump off cliffs with a parachute. And I needed to understand why it was worthwhile.

As I started paring away the layers and thinking about the true nature of my fear, I found myself staring into the eternal conflict between light and dark. Underneath the fear of impending injury or death in the daylight, lies a far deeper fear of being alone. Dark shadows tease the light in an ongoing dichotomy that has bedevilled us since time began. There can never be any real answers to this dichotomy, only half understandings in the dimly lit and dark places of ourselves, places that we seldom venture. Nevertheless, I began a quest for truth, a search for Fear's Holy Grail and I began by looking at Fear's opposite. Courage.

My quest took me back in time. In 480BC a few hundred hand-picked Spartan soldiers were sent to Thermopylae, to defend a narrow pass in the northeast Aegean hills and halt the Persian invasion of Greece. Here, vastly outnumbered, they held back the enemy for three incredible days until they were betrayed by a local resident who showed the Persians a mountain pass that lead behind Greek lines. While the rest of the army fled, King Leonidas, with 300 Spartans and 700 Thespians, held fast, though they knew it meant their own deaths. In one of the most famous last stands in history, they bought time to allow the other Greek troops to withdraw and Athens to prepare herself for battle.

Every single one died in mortal hand-to-hand combat, but one man lived for a few days – long enough to tell the tale of supreme courage against impossible and hopeless odds. His story found its way into the writing of Herodotus and tells of the complex and astonishing sense of brotherhood that existed among the group of soldiers as they fought and died together.

When asked whether they had been afraid, the dying soldier replied that fear, Phobos, is a masculine word, but the camaraderie and kinship that they felt during those days of battle was not masculine at all. As they pushed their phalanx forward and butchered the enemy, inflicting casualties that way outnumbered their own, the overwhelming feeling was that of an inexplicable love towards the fellow soldier fighting next to them. They felt not fear, but community, a love, or a sense of kinship, knowing that they had to stand fast and fight hard to protect their fellow men in the crush of flailing swords and lances. And their brothers were doing the same for them. (Perhaps, too, in the back of their minds, they saw the love in the eyes of their wives as they left Sparta knowing that they would never return, would never again see soft beauty, only iron and blood.) They died loving one another, protecting and honouring their families, their community and their society.

Courage, Andreia, is a feminine word. Instead of fear they felt love, the feminine core of valour. Love is where courage comes from: love is the source of it all.

BASE jumping is like being at war. Beneath the calm, calculating mind control there is a battle raging, war against instinct, against rationality and everything that is soft, gentle and feminine. Not every jump feels like that, most are quite benign. It is only the terrifying ones that feel like being in battle: the ones that we remember because of the speed, the violence and the sharpness. The ones in which fear slices through us like a sword.

Every time I've stood on the edge about to BASE jump, I haven't felt courageous at all, nor have I felt any love, only a chilling sense of aloneness. My choice is free. I could step away at any point. But I don't. I'm not defending my family or my community, I am doing it purely for myself, and yet I have still felt afraid. Why did I keep doing it then?

I think it is because if I don't, it will be worse. If I walked away, it would be so much worse than facing the fear. If I imagine sitting on the beach watching the sky turn purple while the surf breaks onto the rocks with my wife beside me, I recognise it as a sublime moment of peace and tranquillity in the place where I belong. But I also know that I can't be there, and be happy, if I haven't fulfilled that need – the overwhelming desire I have – to see if I can face terror squarely, elbow it aside, and jump off the edge.

Standing before a jump, I prepare myself for death or injury, but I don't want either. Inside me there is a vast, seemingly uncrossable expanse of alienation – from myself and from the people that I love, and who love me. It's a huge and terrifying expanse of existence, a lonely place where no one can help me. It is here that I confront the fear of being alive and alone. Sartre called this place the "hollow centre of being".

And it is something we all face. To avoid this terror, we run away looking for distraction in our work, family, routine, sport, or climbing. Even BASE jumping is a distraction. On the surface, it holds the promise of thrill and adrenaline. The air beyond the edge is familiar because we've all been there before and we know how our bodies will fall. Besides, once we go over there's nothing we can do, we've dispatched ourselves into the hands of gravity, fate, and luck.

But we still have to propel ourselves over the edge, and that's where the uncertainty is. Why are all BASE jumpers afraid on exit point? Some may be calmer than others, but nobody is ever comfortable. We clasp hands, sometimes hugging each other, desperately wanting the community that soldiers feel before going into battle. But in reality we are all utterly and completely alone.

And then we jump and there's nothing more we can do. After the first instant we relax. Our spirits soar free from their mortal constraints and we're suspended for a few seconds in a liminal state, on a threshold, not quite a bird, but not quite a human either, somewhere between heaven and earth. Very much alive. Then we open our parachutes and we're still alive and we land.

Afterwards, once the initial exhilaration has faded, we feel strangely depressed because we only managed to escape for a short while. And it didn't transform us after all that we went through to get there. We had been expecting renewal and nothing happened. We wrote ourselves off and then came back and there was still an abyss in our souls that we hadn't managed to cross.

I have often heard words like "brave" and "courageous" being applied to BASE jumpers, but it's not like that at all. All of us are afraid. There is no visible evidence, but it is eating us alive inside. We are alone and it's terrifying.

In all my climbing, and I've done a lot of climbing completely alone, soloing routes on some of the world's toughest rock and mountains, sometimes with a rope and sometimes without, I've never felt this same sense of terror and aloneness. I have often wondered why that is. Some of it has to do with the concentration that's needed to climb alone, but mostly it's because climbing is an expansive process that draws a person in – you become an intimately connected part of another world as you make your way upwards.

Big wall aid climbing is scary at times, but it is a process with many safeguards: sharp pricks of terror are soothed by long periods of concentration as one engineers a way up the rock. I once spent three days alone on the kilometre-high, sheer granite wall of El Capitan in Yosemite Valley, California, and never once was I afraid. On the third evening, 800 metres above the ground straight below me, I reached the place where I would bivouac for the night. There was no comfy ledge at all, just half a dozen bolts haphazardly sprayed across the yellow rock, lost in a vast ocean of granite, but it was so comforting to see them. Like stepping outside the 300th floor of a skyscraper to sleep on the balcony, I had arrived at my home for the night and my spirit soared.

I set up my portaledge to the comforting clacking sound of aluminium and nylon as it formed itself into my bed for the night. Every so often I would pause and look up (climbers always look upwards, it's the nature of the game. It's only BASE jumpers who look downwards and study the depths of air below), and finally I could see the top not too far off; another few hours and I'd be off the wall. I organised my gear and then I could finally relax the grip of concentration that is like a clamp in every solo climber's mind. I sat on the ledge with my back against the smooth granite wall and dangled my feet over hundreds of metres of air. I took a long pull of warm plastic-tasting water from the water bottle, lit a cigarette and rejoiced in the simple pleasure of where I was, high off the ground, secure, safe, and perfectly at home in the vertical world.

A deep sense of peace came over me, a sense of fulfilment and a profound happiness that I wished I could share with someone, but the closest people were 300 metres below. I could see them preparing their own bivouac.

I didn't feel afraid at all, quite unlike the existential terror that underlies BASE jumping. Although I was completely alone, it didn't seem that way because it felt like I had become an integral part of something that was so much bigger than me. There was a community between myself and nature, I felt like I truly belonged, and it was a comfort to find that the dark shadows inside me had become benign rather than terrifying. Everything felt right, and my soul felt full and satisfied instead of half empty like it always did after each jump.

I lay awake for a long time, calm, comfortable and happy. I felt a deep upwelling of love for this vast world and my small place in it, and a strong affinity for the sharp rough rock that angled so steeply above and below me. I had carried my world up here, and although I was alone, I didn't feel afraid at all. When we embrace the world it gives us the courage to face whatever is still to come. Hanging 800 metres above the ground, I slept the deep sleep of the contented and glad.

That is not always the case, though. In the mountains fear has many faces. There is the terrifying naked vulnerability of being exposed to falling rocks screaming down at you like missiles from above, and there is the heart-stopping icy chill that comes from standing on a snow slope as it slumps just before it avalanches. But by far the cruellest is being caught, helplessly, in an electrical storm high on the side of a peak. Julie and I were climbing the North Face of Mount Alberta in the empty wilds of the Canadian Rockies when I felt firsthand what lay beneath the ragged edge of fear.

It was late in the afternoon and we were heading for an ice field that hung just beneath the summit when we realised we needed to bivouac in a hurry because an electrical storm was gathering its purple and black anger over Mount Robson to the north. Below us dropped 11 long and very vertical pitches of black limestone and below that, 700 metres of ice swept clear to the glacier. There was nowhere flat enough to stand and no solid protection for anchors at all. It would take us all night to chop a ledge in the blue ice above us with our ice axes, so I started mining right where I stood, prying loose piles of rock off the edge. There seemed to be no end to the looseness. In fact, the whole mountain seemed to be a delicately balanced and frozen pile of loose rubble. Presently I manufactured a reasonable place to sit and a little later, I excavated the whole rib into a decent ledge. An ice screw turned squeaking into the ice sheet 30 metres above gave us an anchor and we settled into the simple luxury of being able to lie down on an alpine wall. And what a place! We were high enough to catch a brief shaft of late sunlight fleeing the oncoming storm. It was clear enough to see the Columbia ice fields stretching off to the east, and we had a ringside seat on the cavalry of approaching lightning.

We hunkered down and waited for the storm. It felt like we were the only people left alive as we watched the furious Armageddon approaching. All our metal climbing hardware was hanging on the end of the rope below us and I was worried. I have heard many stories of electrocution by lightning in high places. And then the storm was with us. Two hundred metres above us the summit of Mount Alberta pierced the storm like a lightning rod. The air was alive: buzzing and hissing electricity tickled our noses and ears and static charges arced across everything like sparklers. Snakes of white fire cracked open the sky. The air roared with thunder and wind. Black clouds were driven by violent winds. The sharp smell of cordite punctured the air and I tasted the gritty rockfall dust of fear. Julie and I huddled on the ledge and waited for the explosion that would surely come: for the bolt of lightning that would incinerate us. I wondered if it would hurt. We held hands and waited to die. My heart pounded and I flinched every time the lightning struck and yet I felt completely calm, resigned. There was nothing more we could do, our lives were in the hands of fate. The earth and the sky lashed out at each other in furious combat. The black rock took body blow after body blow of white lightning.

And then gradually the intensity eased as the powerful winds blew the storm past us down the valley, and we could see the wicked flashes of lightning strikes on other peaks. The sleet stopped and the sun came out as we made our dinner and we both laughed with relief. That night I slept deeply with a dreamless contentment that came from our reprieve from an almost certain execution.

The next morning we reached the summit and though I never hang around on summits, we spent an hour on the top despite the tricky, time-consuming and dangerous descent that lay ahead. Across the valley North Twin was close enough to touch. I felt poised on the cusp of the world. There was nothing I couldn't see, nothing to obscure the truths behind the wind, the sky, the snow, the rocks and that pale morning sun. My soul felt unlimited and in a way I felt as close to whatever God there is as I might ever get. There was no place higher but a heaven itself.

It was a deeply personal hour, but also intimately shared because Julie was there. With alpine climbing the partnership of the rope is very close. You're still alone, but there's another presence, another human to help ease the load. Climbing has a community and a kinship that is missing in BASE jumping. There is a profound sense of belonging in a natural world so much bigger than ourselves, and also a deep spiritual affinity with the person with whom it is shared.

We travel across the sharper edges of the world connected by a thin rope, but also connected in the existential void all around us. Climbing embraces so much more because of this shared connection. In it I found the kinship and love of the Spartan soldiers in a different kind of war, in which there is no fear.

What I finally understood is that the opposite of fear is not courage, it is love, and armed with that it's easy to face the darkness.

The fury in the cloud
Becomes an ingredient of the blood
And the spirit's mover.
The road up is the only way:
The soul's source
And the answer to any question.

HOMEWARD BOUND, *ALPINISM VOL I*

Questions

THE CASSIN RIDGE, DENALI, ALASKA

Imagine you have a burning desire to go somewhere. You get out of bed, get dressed and make breakfast, all while squeezed inside a fridge. You go to your car, not knowing whether it will start, whether there is enough fuel to get you where you are going or whether the road ahead will collapse away beneath you. Perhaps the roads themselves will have changed during the night and you don't know if you will find your way or whether a hurricane or snow blizzard will engulf you. You have no idea where you will sleep that night, whether you will finish your journey, and if not, whether you will be able to get back to where you started. Often you don't even know whether you will still be alive tomorrow.

Mountaineering is like this.

We are climbers. Drawn by the beckoning silence of big mountains, our desire is to reach the summit in order to find the answer, once and for all, to the big question of whether we can do it. We start up, burdened by our equipment and carrying a thousand small questions in our heavy packs. Will the weather hold? Will the snow conditions be OK? Will we make it? Mountaineering is about living with uncertain answers to many questions: some will be answered and some won't. And sometimes the answers will come before the questions have been asked.

The endless stream of questions kept coming as Julie and I climbed the Cassin Ridge. The Cassin is a route on Denali, the highest peak in America, which lies deep in the wilderness of Alaska. As we reached a vast snowfield below the summit a surreal halo circled the sun and a thin, fine mist glittered across the sky under high cirrus clouds that looked as if they had been painted in quick, crude brushstrokes. The weather had been fickle until then and the clouds could be warning us that another storm was brewing over the Baring Sea to the southwest. I hoped not. It would have been an awful place to get trapped by a storm.

It was our ninth day on the route and the fourteenth day since we'd left base camp, and we still hadn't reached the top. Above us, a white windblown ridge tilted to the summit, 800 metres higher, while below, peaks and glaciers stretched away into a white wilderness. We were higher than anything else, high on the lonely side of Denali where the air is sharp and freezing cold.

What would we encounter on these final 800 metres? Would we be able to walk on the snow, or would we have to plough a trench up to our waists like we'd done until now? Would our food and gas last? We'd only packed food for eight days and gas for our stove for 10, and both were very nearly finished. Was that enough?

The Cassin Ridge is a beautiful line – it's the quintessential climb of the Alaska Range. It creates a perfect symmetry in the gargantuan expanse of Denali's 3000-metre South Face, sweeping directly to the summit of the largest mountain on the North American continent. At 6150 metres it is one of the most sought-after climbs in the world, a modern test piece and a lasting tribute to the visionary first ascensionists.

First climbed in 1961 by the prolific Italian alpinist, Riccardo Cassin and five companions from the Italian Alpine Club, it proved taxing from the beginning and they battled their way up the ridge, battered by gale force winds and heavy snowfall. Back then it was the golden age of climbing, when the world's mountains and their finest lines were wide open to exploration. But even today, Denali remains a coveted prize. Although the climbing is not that difficult, the long and dangerous approach, 3000 metres of sustained climbing, the high altitude, arctic cold, lengthy storms and difficult retreat have made the Cassin Ridge a serious endeavour.

Of all the people who have climbed the Cassin Ridge, the one I most respect is a slight, bearded man whom I once met on Table Mountain as he scampered effortlessly up the steep rock below the cableway. In 1981 Dave Cheesmond, a South African, soloed the Cassin Ridge in three days and perfect conditions. Even taking good snow conditions into consideration you can't imagine the measure of determination and mental strength it takes to solo a route like the Cassin. He'd even dropped a crampon off his boot from the top of a 300-metre couloir and had to go back to fetch it, before continuing up.

Dave had been the driver behind climbing in South Africa in the 1970s, putting up new routes all over the country. He was also Ed's climbing mentor. But in the end he'd emigrated to Canada, settling in Calgary near the Rocky Mountains, where he printed his name firmly into Canadian climbing legend by climbing hard new routes on the alpine walls of the Rockies. Every time he went climbing he was "training" for something else, something bigger, higher, and steeper. In the end he "trained right over the edge", as Cape Town climber Tony Dick put it. Dave disappeared into the snows of the Yukon on a route called Hummingbird on Mount Logan in Northern Canada. He was with an American woman, Catherine Freer, who was as tenacious as he was. Together they were like bulldogs, they never gave up until the very end. Apparently a cornice collapsed as they were sleeping in their tent, pitching them both into a fatal fall to the glacier many thousands of metres below.

Catherine was Julie's best friend. I never met her because she was killed the year before I met Julie, but they had climbed together for years. In Yosemite Valley in California the pair of them climbed every single crack graded at 5.9 before they felt ready to move on to the next level of difficulty, and that's hard to beat because some of those obscure 5.9 routes are desperately tricky. Julie has very few close friends and Catherine was one of them. They even looked alike. Both had long dark hair and powerful physiques. Julie was distraught for a long time afterwards. She slept with a picture of Catherine next to her bed. Sometimes she would cry, and when I asked she would wipe away the tears, smile, and shake her head saying: "Oh nothing, I'm just thinking about Catherine."

To climb anything successfully in Alaska you have to keep going through good conditions and bad, through starlight and storm. It's a risk you take to get where you want to go. But Dave and Catherine didn't survive to find the answers to the many questions I'm sure they had on that remote and lonely mountain.

Now I can see it, the summit, a faraway point of white against the misty sky. That once distant object has become almost real. My head feels clear and my body feels strong. I feel a tiny stab of adrenaline. For the first time in two weeks I allow myself the pleasure of thinking that finally, maybe, we would do it. Maybe we would actually reach the top. The summit had always seemed such a distant and unattainable object from the Cassin Ridge approach, high up there in the ice and clouds. Suddenly I forgot the thousand curses, the pain and the suffering of the days past. The exhilaration of being so high up, with the summit close enough to touch, gives my legs a burst of energy that leaves my lungs heaving as my crampons bite sharply into the squeaky wind slab snow. For the previous nine days we had thought of nothing but what was immediately before us. All we had done was climb: there had been only the next footstep into bottomless snow and the next axe placement in hard winter ice. We had been suspended in time, high in space. But inside I knew, I was sure. We'd keep going until we reached the top.

Six weeks earlier, Julie and I had stood on the summit we now so coveted. We had started up the West Buttress Route, the easiest way up Denali and the way in which we would descend after Cassin Ridge. It was our first trip to Alaska. As we'd skied up the Kahiltna

Glacier, with big packs and sleds in tow, it was like gliding along the surface of a pool into a new world, a world of snow and ice and arctic temperatures. It was a place in which everything froze solid unless kept close to our bodies inside our bulky clothes, a world in which we were always just a fraction away from frostbite. Our climb had been punctuated by waves of storms that had kept us tent-bound for days: days of waiting and waiting, until finally a window of good weather arrived and we'd climbed to the top.

Now I can visualise that tiny patch of snow that is the top of North America. We had stood there and seen the bamboo stick with a piece of red tape flapping madly in the wind and calculated with apprehension the speed of the approaching storm. Our time on the yellow-tinged summit was like the suspended moment of a ball thrown into the air, as it started to drop we turned and plunge-stepped down from those wind-blasted heights.

Those weeks that we had spent at altitude on the West Buttress, in the rare air of 6000 metres, had acclimatised our bodies for the drudgery we'd face on Cassin Ridge. When we'd started up Cassin, the whole mountain was loaded with new snow through which we ploughed a trench upwards, breaking a trail through the deep soft snow that sometimes reached our waists. It was desperately hard, brutal work. The crippling cold, the big packs and the strenuous exertion became part of our lives. Higher up we climbed into narrow ice runnels, up hard blue ice which glinted like mirrors and shattered with every blow. It was strange rock climbing in such a high, cold place, encumbered as we were by so much clothing and equipment that every move we made on rock, that was really quite easy to climb, felt immensely difficult. At times I felt like an astronaut operating on another planet.

At about 4000 metres we dug a snow hole to escape a maelstrom of wind and snow, and we were locked inside those blue walls of ice for two days while a storm raged outside. It was some time during the storm that a calmness descended on us, an acceptance of where we were. There was only one direction we would go, and that was up. We had a one-way ticket to the summit and en route we would find the answers to any questions that came our way.

Our seventh day was the coldest I have experienced, ever. The coldest winter's days of the Alps or the Himalaya don't begin to compare with that bitter arctic cold. While the weather threw everything it could at us, we doggedly climbed our way through rock bands and up couloirs of ice. A wretched wind rifled through our bulky clothes and robbed us of what little heat we had. My goggles froze inside until it was impossible to see though them. It was also impossible to see without them. My hands and feet were numbed of feeling through the best gear available. That night we bivouacked under a rock tower and the tendrils of cold reached right into my sleeping bag to massage my bones. The thermometer plunged below the lowest possible reading of minus 40 degrees Celsius.

I guess what I am saying is that to succeed on technical routes in Alaska a certain determination is needed, something that drives you to persevere through the cruel conditions and the arduous environment. For Julie and I, we had already crossed that threshold and these conditions had simply become a way of life. The past had gone. The future was unreal. We were simply alive in the immediate moment.

At the end of our ninth day up Cassin, high on an endless snowfield, I finally felt like I had become a part of the mountain. Julie and I had stopped being climbers and become part of the shifting snows. We dug in for our final bivouac, the place where we would spend the cramped and exposed hours of blue twilight that is the Alaskan spring night. We chopped out a platform for the tent, peeled the frozen Gore-Tex fabric of our tent apart, and set it up. By now Julie and I had winter bivouacking perfected. Our attention to the small details had kept us and our equipment functioning in the frozen wastelands. We squashed together inside the tent and wormed our way into our sleeping bags, stuffing our inner boots, water bottles, socks, and other items that we couldn't allow to freeze into our bags. We drank the last of our soup. Now our food was gone, but the stress of conserving food and fuel didn't press so hard anymore. Over the summit and down the other side we had a cache that we had hauled up a month before.

The ice inside the tent walls had grown a few centimetres thicker and the diffuse twilight cast an eerie light inside the yellow walls of the tent. Gusts of wind hammered us and bursts of spindrift shot through the tent zipper, which no longer closed properly because it was frozen useless.

A myriad of fears attacked me as I lay there. Could this be another 10-day Alaskan blizzard? Will we summit? Can we survive a storm without food and almost no fuel? How will these last 800 metres be? How bad will the wind become?

I have always been a worrier and a stream of questions without answers assailed me as I lay in my cramped bed. Sleep came in disconnected snatches like the dreamy world of a schizophrenic and the heavy weight of the future made for vivid and uneasy dreams.

But the twilight changed to pale yellow as the dawn glowed softly in the east. Drifting snow still battered the tent, the wind still rifled across the ridge, but the sky above us was clear. We were ready.

We'll do it now; we'll escape this uncertain world to reach the summit again. We'll keep on going until there are no more questions.

Falling into the Big Picture

It had rained the whole weekend in Cape Town – an unsettled September spring rain – but the sun came out just as I loaded my gear into the truck and drove away. My destination lay to the north, the far north. I was on my way to Norway to BASE jump off some of the world's biggest cliffs, huge rock walls of dark granite that tower above the fjords. One monster cliff in particular, Kjerag, drew me because it had become a compulsory destination for any committed BASE jumper. So of course I had to do it.

I'd had to make a snap decision to leave. In September autumn frontal systems sweep across the North Sea hitting the west coast of Norway with ground-level clouds and rain, so I could only commit to going once I was sure of the weather. There's no point in spending heaps of money that you don't actually have to sit in the rain at the base of a huge cliff in Norway. You can do that in the Cape's Cedarberg range over Easter for a fraction of the cost. So when Sky TV forecast five days of clear weather in northern Europe I bought my ticket with a credit card. I knew I was doing the right thing. Jump first, pay later. Just do it, but don't ever tell the bank.

I had never been to Norway before, but I was compelled by all that is Scandinavia, the fjords, the Vikings, and the legends of trolls that lived in grottoes high up in those huge and unrelentingly vertical walls of rock. I arrived at Cape Town airport as excited as a little kid on the way to a birthday party.

The plane took off and I settled back into travelling mode, that zone when your consciousness half shuts down and hours pass effortlessly by. When I'm travelling I like to quietly watch people. Airports are great for that, especially busy European ones. I try to guess their nationalities, their professions, and where they are going. With a profound sense of detachment I watched everything on my two day trip to the other end of the world. I saw style and beauty in Milan, and waterlogged fields and red-roofed medieval villages as we came in to land at Amsterdam. Here I watched the CNN weather channel on a big-screen TV. It showed clear skies over Norway and I felt a surge of adrenaline. I grinned to myself.

"The Braathens flight to Stavanger leaves in an hour."

While waiting in the departure lounge I took the opportunity to repack my parachute, ready for a long, long freefall over the fjord as soon after landing as I could make my way to the top of that cliff. Shaking it out and folding it neatly, I drew stares from my fellow passengers as it was a rather odd place to pack. After many years of travelling around the world on low budgets, I have become immune to the disdain of the general public. I have had looks of horror while I've cooked and eaten dinner on pavements or bedded down for the night in construction sites or gravel pit quarries. Climbing and BASE jumping have one element in common: both are fringe activities relegated to the margins of mainstream society. They are sports that are healthily populated by extremists, fanatics, and people who don't quite fit in. For me, with one foot in each world, I see remarkable similarities between those who climb and those who jump. There are many shared qualities of intensity, ambition, focus and determination, the same desire to challenge the boundaries of what is possible.

We flew into dense cloud over the North Sea, but a weak setting sun sank into clear skies to the west and the weather looked fine 10 kilometres below me as I anxiously kept an eye on it. The plane landed at Stavanger, a mid-sized town on the southwest coast of Norway and I stepped out into a tiny airport with gleaming blond wood floors.

The Norwegian immigration officer at passport control asked me the reason for my visit.

"Tourist."

His next question astounded me.

"Have you come to jump?"

How could he possibly have known that I was there to jump?

Norway may be the BASE-jumping capital of the world, but I didn't think I looked crazy or deranged. I was neatly dressed and although I had long hair, there was no cross-eyed squint, head rocking, tattoos, or body piercings, the standard uniform of some of the other self-destructive BASE jumpers I knew.

"How did you know I was coming to jump?" I asked.

In the musical, lilting way that Scandinavians speak English, the passport officer explained with a smile that it was his job to observe people, much as I had done while travelling, and that I fitted his profile of a BASE jumper. My intentions were clearly too transparent. It reminded me of the time I had walked all the way up the Eiffel Tower in Paris late one evening. A security guard had pinned himself to me, watching my every move, and I never got the chance to jump.

"Do I look crazy?"

"No, you look normal, but now I know you're insane," he laughed as he snapped my passport shut.

"Have a good trip."

I was excited as I walked through Stavanger, heading for the docks past neatly painted clapboard houses, cedar and birch trees and brilliant green grass. I saw modern Vikings: beautiful blonde women and strong ruddy-faced men. I saw an affluent society where new cars drove across centuries-old cobbled streets. A young cobbler was hard at work using a laser levelling device to lay stones on the road, as the past merged seamlessly with the present. At the ferry terminal I saw the open sea beyond. It was easy to imagine the Vikings of a thousand years ago taking to sea as the same cold wind cut across the fjords.

I boarded a ferry for Lysefjord, a long arm of sea that creeps into the heart of Norway and up to the great cliffs. As the ferry plied deeper into the fjord, the stiff north wind blew clouds across the sky, the sun flashing through gaps in the flying clouds. There was an autumn chill to the air, bringing stern hints of the brutal northern winters. The half-dozen tourists and I scuttled into the cabin to escape the wind and the spray.

In the cabin I met another BASE jumper. I'd noticed a young, attractive woman with a striking grey lock cleaving her thick bob of dark hair, and I'd thought she was a tourist until I saw the Vertigo label on her backpack, the unmistakable brand of a BASE equipment manufacturer. Jill Nettle was a compact South African skydiver who had recently started BASE jumping. She lived in Colorado, USA. A few months before, her American boyfriend, Clint, had been killed in a plane crash in Utah. She had come to Norway because they had long planned to jump here and she felt she owed it to Clint to fulfil their plans all the same. I could see she was grieving his death and she played a very tight hand with herself. There was a self-sufficiency and a hardness to her that thinly concealed her vulnerability, but she gradually warmed to me and in another time and place I could easily have fallen for her.

I thought it astonishing that two South Africans, and BASE jumpers at that, could meet by chance. There were only eight other BASE-jumping South Africans and I knew them all.

The ferry chugged its way up the Lysefjord, finally reaching the small hamlet of Lysebotn. We disembarked to discover that we were the only BASE jumpers there. In the short months of summer Lyse-botn becomes a magnet for jumpers: people from all over the world congregate to fall off the cliffs, and in the babble of languages the common word is freefall. But weeks of rain before our arrival had driven everybody southward and the elderly Norwegian couple who ran the camp site were packing up to leave. We persuaded them to stay open a few days longer because we really wanted to jump and we had come so far. They relented and Ivar, the husband, good-naturedly volunteered to fetch us in his little boat from the landing area after we had jumped. It was two kilometres back down the fjord and accessible only by water.

Dark cliffs towered over the gloomy fjord, and together with the black clouds, it created a sombre atmosphere. It was hard not to feel just a little intimidated.

At 7pm, exactly 48 hours after leaving South Africa, I stood with Jill on the top of Kjerag. The exit point was a prow of rock rounded like the top of a mushroom, which leaned gently further and further over the edge, until it ran out into pure air. There was an hour to go until dark.

Jill and I had marched across alpine meadows for two hours to get to the top, past lichen-covered boulders and big-horned sheep. We had been caught in a rain shower and both of us were soaked, but our parachutes were dry because we'd carefully wrapped them in black plastic bags inside our packs. It had taken effort, money, and a substantial amount of travelling to get there.

I felt my senses sharpening as I strapped on my parachute and looked over the edge: it plunged straight down to the inky blue water of the fjord a vertical kilometre below. Gravity and water are powerful forces in Norway, like the ice that had inexorably carved these immense walls of granite. I stood on top of that jutting rock, just a flash of human life against an age of geologic time. It made me feel very small, like the jump I was about to do, a fleeting burst of human energy lost in the enormity of human existence.

All around us were dark granite cliffs, huge in their sheerness, echoing legends of trolls, goblins and monsters that lurked in their fissures. Now that I was there the myths seemed plausible and they added to the tension in the air. Below was an emerald green grassy landing area next to a small lighthouse that warned boats against the rocky headland jutting out into the fjord.

I straightened up. Distant rays of sunlight dotted the water. Lysebotn village lay quaintly at the head of the fjord, before an intensely green valley. Everything seemed toy-sized. But foremost in my senses was the yawning blue abyss five steps beyond. I felt completely calm.

"Have a good jump," I said. Jill seemed calm too. She has a strong head and nerves of steel, but all the best people do. Perhaps it's that focus?

Then, without another thought, I ran off the edge.

From 1000 metres above the fjord, with my head held high to watch the horizon, I dropped. The feeling was of pure ecstasy. I was free, released from the boundaries of this earth. The acceleration was explosive. I swept my arms back and after six seconds I felt myself start to fly. At 12 seconds I plunged through the air like an arrow. The colour around me was a whirl of black, blue and green.

I had found that state of grace once again: those precious moments of infinity, where subject and object become one and where you simply are. It was my paradise, like sex for some or a drug-induced high for others. There is nothing in the world to compare with the sensation of freefalling, tracking down towards the earth at 200 kilometres per hour.

Then I swept my arms forward again into a flare for another second. I watched the ground rushing up at me and then I threw my pilot chute to the wind and my canopy opened cleanly, its green and yellow colours etched against the tall dark cliffs hundreds of metres above. I felt absolutely alive, as if life itself were something tangible like a coat that I had put on to take away the cold. I turned out over the water and landed hard and fast on the small beach at the base of the cliff. The canopy deflated and I looked up at Kjerag, an immense, forbidding bastion of dark granite.

Jill jumped after me and she landed safely next to the lighthouse with a huge grin. Her hands shook as we gave each other a high-five.

But then it was almost as if it had never happened. It was the strangest thing.

Afterwards, as we rode in the little boat with its whining outboard motor back to Lysebotn I felt as if I hadn't jumped at all. It was only the unpacked parachute in the stash bag between my knees that was evidence of what we had done. Our jump had been like a wisp of cold northern cloud on an autumn evening, one minute it's there and the next it's gone.

For a few seconds I had been flying, free from mortal constraints. That was my state of paradise, escape perhaps, but no different to the state reached when someone absorbs a beautiful place. This was just a different way of looking at the same thing. The rest of what we do is distraction, a smokescreen shielding us from the bigger picture – that chilly vision of one's transience in a cruel and beautiful world and the briefness of our passing through it.

Everybody tries to build something constructive and tangible. We work so hard to make our lives the way we want them, but everything we do is so temporary. Disappointments, setbacks, sorrow and pain accrue like interest on a home loan, building up to follow us around like the small kitten that trailed Jill and I as we walked around Lysebotn in the rain the day after our jump. What really keeps us going are the connections with the people we love, those brief moments of joy in an otherwise epic struggle.

It all became obvious that the depressing meaninglessness I was feeling was because BASE jumping is a solitary experience and worthless unless you share it. But there is no way to share it. When you face it alone, the future is appalling. But when you share life's experiences with others, the future builds hope, and there is a solidarity and meaning to it all. It's all about growing up. Sometimes we need to go to the edge and beyond, into a brief spell of madness, to discover the simplest things.

A week later, well after midnight, I trudged through Stavanger, passing beautiful blonde women spilling out of nightclubs. I was southbound this time, headed for home via warm sunny crags and more high cliffs in Europe. I walked over the cobblestones the cobbler had laid, a little wiser now, with a clearer vision of who I was in this far-off part of the world.

Then I laid out my sleeping bag in a construction site near the airport and wrapped myself up tightly against the chilly September night.

Some things don't change much in the bigger picture.

The challenge of peaks is the challenge of life itself, to struggle ever higher. Challenge is what makes great men and there can be no challenge without the risk of failure.

PHIL SNYDER, ONE-TIME
WARDEN ON MOUNT KENYA

In the Throne Room of the Mountain Gods

Imagine you are climbing a tree. A big tree. You climb up the trunk and then, when you are really high, you tentatively move out along a branch that gets thinner and weaker the further you go. The branch begins to bend and wobble. Your pulse races and palms get slippery. Pretty soon you get to point where you're loath to go on. The branch creaks ominously, the ground's a deadly distance below.

Beyond this point there is a chance you won't be able to get back to safety, that this could cost you your life.

You are completely extended and strung out – on a limb in the wind.

And then you summon all your mettle and move out into the death zone.

That's what high-altitude alpine climbing is like.

And sometimes you win, sometimes you lose

Gasherbrum IV stands in the middle of a long chain of the world's highest peaks, in the Karakorum; that part of the central Himalayas straddling the border between Pakistan and China, on the roof of the world. It's a beautiful mountain, a mountaineer's mountain with a classic symmetry that is mesmerising. It's known as the shining mountain, because of the way the West Face glows in the evening light, like a mountain on fire. And when you're up there, inside it all, you're on fire too. The emotion is so powerful it's almost like falling in love.

G4 is also huge, hard and terrifying. There are no easy routes on the peak: it's steep and sheer on all sides and very difficult to climb. But that's why we were there: to see if we were equal to the monumental challenge. It would be the most difficult thing any of us had tried and there was no guarantee of success. It's a mountain that could easily break your heart.

For our expedition leader, Steve Swenson, (with whom I had climbed in Alaska) it would be his fourth attempt at conquering this peak. Steve is an internationally respected high-altitude phenomenon and one of a hard-core elite of less than a dozen people who have summited both Everest and K2 without oxygen, both of which he did via their notoriously difficult North Ridges. You could call it an obsession with G4, because collectively he had dedicated an entire year of his life to the mountain, relentlessly trying to reach the summit. A man of laser-like focus, great patience and bullish tenacity, he had spent two years planning this expedition in finicky detail. This time he was determined not to fail.

But we were going against heavy odds. In the 50 years prior to our attempt, only three teams had made it to the top, and precisely seven men had stood on the elusive summit. At a height of 7925 metres, G4 has a well-earned reputation for invincibility, a solitary and impregnable fortress flanked by four towering 8000-metre peaks – its celebrity neighbour, K2, the world's highest peak after Everest, Gasherbrum I, Broad Peak and Gasherbrum II (ranked eleventh, twelfth and fourteenth respectively). G4 comprises flint hard, compact marble rock that offers little in the way of secure protection. The climbing is gruelling, dangerous, and very high. It's up in the Death Zone, that altitude around 8000 metres where there isn't enough oxygen to sustain life for longer than a few days. It's a deadly world that we can pass briefly through, but never inhabit.

And we were going to climb this mountain fortress in alpine style, which means that instead of scurrying up and down laying camps and fixed ropes, we were going up in one continuous push from bottom to top. We'd carry all our gear and food with us, laying some ropes as we went, resting where we could, and then cutting loose into the thin branches of risk and uncertainty.

To climb alpine style on the world's biggest peaks is probably one of the most difficult, uncertain and dangerous things you can do. In the words of Doug Scott, the famous British Himalayan veteran whose narrow escapes on Everest and the Ogre have become mountaineering legend: "You have to write yourself off. You have to tell yourself that you might not come back."

Even so, we had a lot going for us. Steve had gathered the strongest team I've ever climbed with. Together we had the skill and experience to have as good a chance of reaching the summit as anyone and we all had a burning and uncompromising desire to get there. But at high altitude it only counts for so much. The rest is sheer luck. We knew that.

Six weeks before our summit attempt, we landed in the heat and chaos of Islamabad. It was intoxicating: the vibrancy, heady smells and babbling exotic language amid the Third World squalor. Over the next few days I wandered the filthy streets of Rawalpindi, wading through searing air to help our expedition cook, Ghulam Rasool, collect supplies to sustain us over three long, energy-sapping months in the mountains. As we gathered grainy rice in rough-textured bags and haggled over pots and lanterns, I kept thinking about the climb that lay ahead. Would the weather cooperate? Was the mountain really as evasive as I'd heard? Would we all stay healthy at that altitude? Would we get to the top? How would our team pull together?

Days later, as we loaded a mountain of gear onto the rickety Bedford bus with bald tires that would carry us out onto Karakorum Highway, I looked around at my team mates, who were all American. There was Steve, our expedition leader, good looking, efficient and orderly, eyes calculating as he made sure everything was with us and neatly stowed on the bus. A civil engineer by profession, he'd hand picked each of us with the same thought and attention to detail that he'd applied to all the complex logistics. He has an extraordinary mix of qualities, he's gentle but has an unwavering, focused ambition, he's safely conservative and yet extraordinarily bold, a natural leader but also inclusive and democratic.

Then there was Steve House, bouncing in excitement and tossing duffel bags up onto the bus like they're made of polystyrene. We nick-named him the Energizer Bunny. Looking at him you wouldn't know that he was one of the best mixed climbers in the world. With talent as boundless as his energy, Steve calls Washington State his home and is a mountain guide by profession. He's carved new routes into brittle Alaskan and Canadian ice that have certainly earned my respect.

And then suddenly everybody burst out laughing as Charley Mace cracked one of his acerbic and witty one-liners about the wheels on the bus going round and round, until they fell off. He's hilarious. Exceptionally tall, rail thin, and cut from the most unlikely looking mountaineering material. I would have guessed him to be a computer geek instead of a fine mountaineer and Himalayan veteran with some impressive 8000-metre summits under his belt, including K2 and Makalu. Charley and I hit it off immediately.

And then there was me. It's a long way from the sunny crags of Table Mountain to G4, but I was there for my rock climbing experience in high places. While I had done technical routes all over the world, the highest I had been was 7000 metres on an unsuccessful attempt at the unclimbed North Ridge of Latok II in Pakistan a few years before.

Finally we were on our way, after two years of preparation. The bus, which was adorned with medallions, badges and paraphernalia to ward off the dangers of travel, would carry us for 40 hours to Skardu, where we'd get onto dusty jeeps to head into the mountains to Askole.

Inshallah, we will arrive safely.

From Askole we started the 10-day trek up to our base camp using the broad reaches of the giant Baltoro Glacier, that big river of ice draining off K2, Broad Peak, and G4, as a footpath. It was hard going as our expedition caravan snaked up the rough terrain. With us were the 100 tough, leathery Balti men we had hired as porters who were carrying everything we needed on their strong backs.

It was no mean task. Aside from our expedition gear we were also carrying portable toilets to place in the once pristine camp sites on the Baltoro Glacier. A popular trekking route, it had become quite unhygienic in recent years and to this end Steve had persuaded corporates and grant agencies to donate a large amount of money to our expedition, ostensibly named the 1999 Gasherbrum Environmental Expedition. In reality, what we were really doing was carrying plywood toilet boxes that we called Thrones into the mountains.

On the fourth day we crested the terminal moraine and clambered up onto the Baltoro glacier to our first view of the mountain and everyone fell silent. Thirty kilometres away G4 rose up like a juggernaut.

"Fucking hell!" said House.

"Yowza!" said Charley.

I said nothing. It was a sobering moment.

G4 looked immense. Taller and steeper than I could have ever imagined, it towered up into the pale blue sky. Our route looked huge and daunting. We had come to climb the South West Ridge, which isn't really a ridge at all, but a slab that towered 3000 metres from the glacier to the summit, nearly three kilometres into the air. Two of G4's ridges and three of its faces are still unclimbed and it was easy to see why. It looked like a hard mountain even to our experienced eyes.

With these sombre thoughts we were all silent as we carried on up the glacier. I knew that the other guys were feeling just as sober as I was. For the rest of the approach I couldn't keep my eyes off the mountain. We kept making light of it. Steve House, in his slow western drawl, joked about how our expedition had "return postage guaranteed" stamped all over it because we would stay until we had climbed it, even if it meant doing the first winter ascent.

In early July we reached our base camp at 4800 metres on the moraine atop the upper reaches of the Abruzzi Glacier. From there we would set up a camp on the upper Gasherbrum glacier at about 6000 metres and acclimatise our bodies to the altitude by rallying back and forth carrying food, fuel and equipment up to this camp. Beyond that, we would set up another camp on the crest of the ridge overlooking the west face. When it came to our summit push, we would cut loose from here and climb alpine style to the top. This seemed the safest and most efficient way to climb the route.

And so we set to work. From our comfortable base camp with tables and chairs, music, books and fresh coffee, it was a 15-kilometre convoluted slog up through the creaking, jumbled ice fall, and then a steep ascent on our skis along the slopes of the Upper Gasherbrum Glacier to our camp at 6000 metres. On these days we'd get up at 2am and, clad in heavy down jackets to keep out the cold, we would leave base camp to climb through the icefall by headlight torches, reaching the upper glacier at dawn. Then we would clip into our skis on the upper glacier and arrive at our first camp at 10am before the sun turned the bowl into a fiery white oven as we slept in the shade of our tents. I bunked with Charley and the two Steves shared a tent. In the late afternoon, after the sun dipped behind G5, the temperature would plunge 60 degrees or more, from plus 30 to minus 30. It was a high, wild, white desert of extremes.

And it was incredibly hard work. Even breathing was a struggle in the thin air as we ground our way up ever-steeper slopes with big packs. Charley was convinced that he would be a pack mule in his next life with all the training he was getting. Sometimes my mind wandered and I would be released from the pain of the physical exertion. Sometimes I couldn't find this release and I was trapped inside my own suffering. But always I had to focus upwards as exertion and rest blended into one with fatigue, and day followed day. We were like tiny ants in the shadow of this great peak as we carried our loads through the icefall and prepared for our ascent.

But up there, standing on that remote glacier, it truly felt like we were in the throne room of the mountain gods. In a horseshoe-shaped sweep around us, the snowy flanks of Gasherbrums I (Hidden Peak) and II, soared skywards on the right, with Gasherbrums V and VI on the left. And then, rising centre stage directly in front of us was G4, bigger, sharper and steeper than ever from close up, despite the foreshortening effect of being directly underneath it. Two thousand metres above us, the wind blew a crested plume of snow off the summit. It was a beautiful, intimidating and invigorating place to be.

Standing there in a brisk and freezing wind one afternoon, I thought about the select few who'd succeeded in climbing this mountain. The first was my boyhood hero, that visionary Italian mountaineer Walter Bonatti, who'd hammered a final peg into the top of the peak in 1958, as he summited with Carlo Mauri. It was my dream to touch that peg, which is still there today, testimony to their bold and skilful climb up the North East Ridge.

It would be 28 years before G4 was summited again in 1986, by Australians Greg Child and Tim McCartney-Snape and the American Tom Hargis. And they found Bonatti's peg. The year before though, in 1985, an attempt was made that was arguably the most audacious and boldest ever made, when the Pole Voytek Kurtyka and the Austrian Robert Schauer completed the finest climb ever done in the Himalayas. Climbing the West Face in pure alpine style, they started without fixed ropes and carrying all their own food and equipment on their backs, and climbed the staggering three-kilometre-high wall in one continuous push. By the time they reached the intersection with the North East Ridge they were totally strung out, having been without food for six days and without water for three. They were both hallucinating badly. Schauer kept seeing himself as a raven circling and looking down at his own shrivelled body curled up in the snow below. They realised that if they didn't get down they would almost certainly die up there and so they descended the unknown northeastern ridge, which would only be climbed the following year by the Australian/American team. They barely got down with their lives.

Their attempt would bring them wide acclaim in climbing circles, but it was not enough and Kurtyka would decry the attempt as his greatest failure. "How can you go back when you have played out your life so close to the edge and returned unfulfilled?"

Finally in 1997 two members of a large team of Koreans would summit the Central Spur on the West Face with martial efficiency and 4000 metres of fixed rope. Seven people is a scant number of climbers to have made it to the top, considering that Gasherbrum II and Hidden Peak have had hundreds of ascents simply because they are above 8000 metres.

Julie used to liken climbing big peaks to eating an elephant – you have to take one bite at a time. We took many small steps, each one taking us higher and higher, as our bodies slowly acclimatised to working in the thin air. It took us three weeks of hard labour before we were ready to start up the big ice wall. It's 1000 metres high, the same height as Table Mountain but sheer, and it leads up to the crest of the ridge at 7100 metres.

Here we strung 600 exhausting metres of rope to protect ourselves from the avalanches that regularly swept down the face in bad weather. At night we collapsed into the lopsided tents that we'd had to drape, saddle-like, over the ridge, with sheer drops into the void on either side. Here we slept to acclimatise, trying to ignore the roar of the wind blasting the summit into a continual plume of snow. It sounded like a fleet of jet planes taking off and was a constant reminder of the severity of the challenge that lay ahead.

I really wanted to climb this mountain. I was spellbound by its beauty, and besotted with the fact that it was almost insurmountable. It is vertical on all sides and there is no easy way up. I've always liked challenging climbs on aesthetic lines with a high factor of uncertainty. G4 epitomises what the "art of climbing" is all about. On difficult peaks the line between success and failure is so razor thin that climbing becomes a form of art. The only thing that would tip success into our favour would be the emotions that we bring with us, emotions like desire, self-denial, ambition, or as Steve House once said, "The want-it factor".

But the weather wasn't playing on our side. Snow storms would blow in and dump fresh snow onto the ice wall, making it dangerous to climb as the new snow sloughed off in big avalanches that billowed down the ice. In addition, Steve Swenson was sick a lot of the time with a hacking cough and stomach bug. His insides turned to liquid, but still he kept eating, packing in more than came out, determined to stay strong. The Third World virus that had befallen him played havoc with his sinuses. At night he would snore like a clutch of Harley Davidson bikes out on a rally, until it got so bad that he'd wake himself up, but his eyes never left the summit.

Six weeks after starting out, we'd reached that stage of our climb where we would now leave the comfort of our base and head out along that thin and perilous branch into that tenuous other world. I saw Charley stuff a picture of his brand new baby boy deep into his pocket before we left.

We started by climbing into the rock bands. I felt as mobile as a stuffed turkey clad in my bulky Michelin Man down suit, carrying a full rack of mountain-climbing hardware and a pack that weighed maybe 12 or 13 kilograms, containing all my gear. Climbing that should have been easy felt difficult. I lurched and scrabbled desperately. My ice axes dangled from my wrists and my crampon points bit into sloping rock covered with fresh snow. The route finding was complex and the rock was tricky, either polished and featureless or loose.

The higher we pushed the more laboured my breathing became. Down below it is impossible to imagine what it is like to fight for every breath, but up there, there is never enough air. I would make a strenuous move and plunge into oxygen deficit as I panted to suck it in, my breathing sharp and shallow. The air tasted strangely metallic, as if the oxygen had been replaced by heavy mercury that settled in my legs and made my head ache. I felt like a 96-year-old war veteran.

At this altitude the air in which we were climbing has less than half the oxygen we get at sea level. And it's not enough. To cope your heart beats faster, your body shuts all non-essential functions so your digestive system barely works and you battle to sleep. And then there is the risk of pulmonary or cerebral oedema, a potentially deadly risk that can befall anyone, which occurs when your body is rendered un-able to extract water in your tissues through normal capillary action, allowing these fluids to collect in a deadly pool in your lungs or brain.

Oedema usually comes with too rapid acclimatisation, but it can befall a strong, fit climber who has flu, bronchitis or any other minor illness. It is a tenuous business staying alive at the top of the world.

Even the Energizer Bunny found it hard going. I could see him sucking air like a drowning man. Together we switched leads and after a few pitches I forgot where I was because all my focus was on the next protection and anchor in the loose and compact rock. Loose snow coated rotten slabs. I hammered in a bad peg and clipped the rope into it anyway. It would never have held a fall. Another ledge loomed and more panting. I felt very tired. The climbing was slow, tedious and precarious, but the pitches unfolded higher and higher, fitting together like an intricate puzzle in the cold air.

That night we bivouacked on a small, down-sloping ledge, pitching our two tiny tents and squashing ourselves inside. The South East Ridge had long since merged into the West Face and we were stranded between vast slabs of steep pink rock above us and the vertiginous climbing below. We brewed tea on our stove and dozed while we waited for it to boil. The boiling point at that altitude was only lukewarm, and we had to rest in between gulps. We tried to eat the dehydrated meal packs we had brought, but not one of us was hungry. "Why the hell did we bring this food up anyway?" asked Charlie as it took him five minutes to swallow a mouthful of beef stroganoff. I had a bite of an energy bar and tried to sleep, but it felt like someone was trying to suffocate me. So I just lay there in a stupor, not quite awake, but not really asleep either.

It was a precarious and precious place to be, perched high up on the edge of the West Face. K2 and Broad Peak shadowed our fitful and vivid hypoxic dreams like monsters, while the ragged Baltoro stretched away far below, a chaotic and jumbled river of ice. We were in a truly special place, unimaginably wild and savage, but it possessed a quiet white peace that placated our pounding hearts and heaving lungs. There was a remoteness and a disconnection that I felt when I looked down the thousands of icy metres to where the rest of the world lay below. I was stranded, suspended in time on the jagged edge of the earth.

The next morning it was snowing and very windy. None of us wanted to be trapped on the mountain in a storm, and the conditions were worsening by the minute. All of us agreed that it would be impossible to continue. We were forced to make the sensible choice and go all the way back down to base camp. We were exhausted.

For three weeks straight we were plagued by southern winds that blew in from India, bringing clouds and snow, heralding the perimeter of the monsoon. It stormed and then snowed and then cleared again, and then it rained. The weather was fickle and we couldn't predict it. The uncertainty became unbearable as we rode an emotional roller coaster, vacillating between wanting to go home and the desire to summit.

One afternoon Steve unzipped my tent as I lay reading David Guterson's *East of the Mountains*, and said: "Hang in there. This will pass. I know it's hard." He was a sensitive leader and he'd seen all of this before. We ran out of books to keep us occupied, and we spent several days trying to decipher the words of songs by The Catheters, an awful sounding punk band lead by Steve's 18-year-old son, Jasper. I felt exasperated by the weather.

And still we kept on trying to go up – to second guess the weather. We even ascended the icefall in a blizzard, until it got so wild and so bad that we were forced to turn around. We spent five days pinned in camp one while a metre of snow buried our tents. It was claustrophobically boring with nothing to do except lie in the tent. Even Charley ran out of jokes and we were running out of time. All the other expeditions had left the mountains and the season was drawing to a close.

Charley was missing his baby boy at home in Colorado. "I'm bailing out," he said one afternoon in base camp as 30 centimetres of new snow lay thick on the glacier outside, "I'm not going up there again." When he said that I very nearly bailed as well. Charley could have left with one of the departing expeditions, but he chose to hang around in base camp to give us moral support.

Two days before we were all due to leave, the China winds howled in from the north, heralding a high-pressure system that brought the good and stable weather for which we had waited so long. The Balti people have two simple ways of predicting the weather: an India wind from the south is bad and a China wind from the north is good. Both Steves and I went up again on a cold clear morning for our last attempt, up through the icefall to camp one and then all the way up to camp two the following day. There was a full moon that night; a ghostly bleached white sphere that made me feel like I was hallucinating, it was so unreal. The snow glowed a cold, crystal grey outside and the temperature plummeted. I felt like I was suspended between two worlds, the world of possibility below and the world of pain and isolation above, and yet I was detached from both.

Both Steves were sick in the night, vomiting up what little food they had eaten, and they both felt grim and weak. Dawn broke as icy mare's tail clouds covered the Indian sky to the south and we all knew the weather would soon change for the worse again. We looked at each other wordlessly and then turned our eyes back to the sky. The good weather had lasted only two days and we needed at least six to get up and down. Steve House optimistically reckoned that we would only need 16 hours to get to the top, but Steve Swenson shook his head and said: "It's not going to happen. We're finished here." Secretly I was relieved. The roller-coaster weather ride of the past three months had left me drained and ambivalent.

That night, lying in my tent in camp one I thought how all of our efforts and ambitions had hinged on one day; one short moment in the great scale of our lives. A different set of chance circumstances would have had us on the summit the following day, but instead we were going home. We hauled all of the equipment back down the mountain as the clouds thickened with snow. Early on the morning that we were to trek out, I went back up to camp one on my own to collect the last of our gear. It was a strange experience to be completely alone in the mountains. All the other expeditions had left weeks earlier and the base camps of K2 and Broad Peak were deserted. I skied up the glacier in a light snowfall, happy not to be able to see G4.

I was angry. I felt like an unrequited lover spurned by the most beautiful woman on earth. We had come so close and yet had no opportunity to stake our claim on the summit. How I had dreamed of seeing Bonatti's peg! How I had wanted to see forever through the high clear air up there! I collected the bag and skied back down to the icefall, full of disquiet.

As we trekked out in appalling weather, Steve Swenson calmed me by saying that as he got older the disappointment didn't eat away at him so much any more.

"It's all about humility," he said, "I just don't let it chew me up so much anymore." I was amazed that someone who had spent so long trying to climb this mountain could accept failure with such an even philosophy. But then he was finished with G4, or so he said. We were all mentally and physically burnt out. We needed gentle places away from the harshness of the snow and ice and rock that we'd been immersed in for so long.

Eventually my anger turned to a deep disappointment because there really was nothing more we could have done. We had tried hard and we had still failed. We could so easily have climbed Gasherbrum II or Hidden Peak by their normal routes. While we were struggling on G4, 11 people from other expeditions climbed G2, people with whom we had shared base camp and cups of tea, but that's not why we went there. We were trying to forge a new route on uncertain ground, and in so doing the great scale of those peaks had become familiar to us because we were right up close, holding small handholds with gloved hands, instead of trudging up a trail of boot prints in the snow.

But even so, I felt a great, unfulfilled desire, like a broken heart. I felt inconsolable. The only thing that can ever ease it, says Steve, is time.

Failure is always hard to accept. It really sets you back – it puts you on your knees for a while and it's with a profound reluctance that I admit to becoming a stronger person because we did not summit. Perhaps we needed to be reminded of our humility in the face of these huge mountains.

Perhaps it's the only way we could have made sense of it all. And perhaps it's good to fail.

But then, as Reinhold Messner, the first person to have climbed all 14 of the 8000-metre peaks has always said: "Summits are important." And that's the uncomfortable rub, like an itchy spot on your back that you just can't seem to reach.

Time dulls the itch, but it never really goes away.

Stages of Women

My wife Charlotte is a sports freak. Usually it's the man in the family who scours the newspaper sports pages and sits glued to the TV during games, but with us it's the other way around. Charlotte is an athlete, a marathon runner, and she's built for the open road like a human greyhound. There is a wild streak in her that I fell in love with, but she's not a fitness addict by any means, it's just that she likes running, and is passionate about sport in general. It's her way of taking time out.

During her pregnancy with our first child, if you looked at her from behind you couldn't tell she was expecting. It was only when she turned sideways that you saw it: a belly on legs. She ran every morning, day in and day out, no matter whether the sun was shining or whether it was pouring with rain. As her belly swelled she started getting odd looks from passing motorists and towards the end, when she began to get really big, people even stopped their cars and asked whether she wanted a lift home. But she waved them all on and carried on running.

Every evening she would squeeze herself and the belly into a wet-suit and go surfing in the ocean. It got to be quite uncomfortable paddling out with a huge stomach, but apparently it used to settle in squashed off to one side, while both of them rode the waves. For a while I got very nervous. I imagined our child developing a brain like spaghetti from the constant pounding on the road and becoming hideously stunted from the icy Atlantic seawater, but the doctor reassured me that the baby would be fine. It was inside a sac full of water, he said, perfectly comfortable and impervious to everything that went on outside. And to her credit, Charlotte did have a very good diet, so I let it run with a shrug of my shoulders and a "healthy mom makes for a healthy baby" attitude.

Our little boy, Sebastian, was born just after a surf one Sunday morning. I think he'd had enough of the sports by then and decided to get out. We got to the hospital just in time and after a short labour, out he popped, healthy, happy, and much to my relief, perfectly normal.

When, two years later, Charlotte became pregnant with our second child it was all old hat to me. She still ran every morning and surfed every evening. The motorists who had seen her on the first round didn't even slow down anymore, but as her belly grew it was she who slowed down. Running at eight months pregnant is hardly running because it's more like a slow jog. Her back ached, her feet hurt, but still Charlotte kept at it and inside her our baby kept on growing.

Three weeks before her due date, she went to bed on a Friday night complaining of an unusually sore back. I thought nothing of it because there was still a while to go, so I turned over and went to sleep. In retrospect, I should have seen the writing on the wall in huge letters reading: "It's a weekend, near the end of her term, so watch out!", but I been at a party that evening and my vision was a little blurry from the whisky.

At 5:20am I woke up to a frantic pounding on the door and the voice of a man shouting in blind panic, "Wake up! Your wife's having a baby. Wake up!" He also rang the doorbells of both our neighbours' houses for good measure. "Help! Somebody! I need help out here!"

Charlotte hadn't been able to sleep that night. She tossed and turned and the pain in her back got worse, but her contractions hadn't started, so she figured it was just the sore back that had plagued her for some time. At 3am she went downstairs and put on her running shoes, twisting sideways around the belly to tie the laces, and then she headed off to run on the deserted road that winds along the sea. It was a clear, starry night in mid-winter, but the night was mild and the air was fairly warm as she trotted along in the dark.

Five kilometres out she felt herself go into labour, so she turned around and started jogging back. Then the contractions really kicked in and she could barely walk in between the heaves of pain. Once it's time for a baby to be born, there's nothing you can do to stop it. The process is irreversible. That's why women give birth on buses, airplanes, in mealie fields and all kinds of strange places, but I had never heard of a woman giving birth on a run before. For some women their labour is long and protracted, but Charlotte was fit and healthy and Sebastian had been born only four hours after she went into labour. As the second child's labour is generally half as long as the first, she knew this one would be quick and she didn't have much time.

The road was deserted. Charlotte stumbled along whispering for me to come and help, but I was fast asleep some way off, immune to the epic that was unfolding. For one and a half hours she walked in between the contractions, convinced that she was going to have to deliver the baby on the side of that dark and lonely road all by herself. At last headlights appeared in the distance and she flagged the car down by standing in the middle of the road waving frantically. Luckily for her it was Scarborough Security Service, which patrols our village in little red cars, monitoring the neighbourhood and offering armed response. The driver, a young man by the name of Johan Esterhuizen, was on his way to fill up his car with petrol and it was pure luck that he happened to be passing at that time of night. Charlotte climbed in and very nearly gave birth right there on his front seat. Johan was clearly out of his depth because delivering babies was quite a stretch beyond his normal job of chasing intruders, but, with wide eyes, he floored the car and made it back to our house in record time. He jumped out and started pounding on doors and ringing bells and he managed to wake up everyone rather sharply.

I raced outside just as Charlotte walked through the gate into our garden: "Andy, it's coming. Now."

She took a few more steps onto the grass and I barely managed to get her running shorts off before the head appeared. An Irish couple, Rees and Jo Kavanagh, who were holidaying in the house next to ours, arrived during all the commotion with flashlights and, along with the now shell-shocked Johan, they all shone their torches as Charlotte squatted down and gave a final push.

Our daughter Clea slid out and landed in my hands, a tiny little thing, all curled up, bloody, blue and covered in vernix wax with the umbilical cord wound tightly around her neck, strangling her. I didn't even hesitate. I grabbed the rubbery cord and pulled it, stretching it like a hard elastic band as it squeaked with tension over her head and then unwinding it so she could breathe. Rees found a pair of scissors and a couple of towels and I cut the cord, setting Clea free, and in that moment she started her life on earth right there in the garden under a pale quarter moon.

There were no choruses of angels or joyful ringing of bells, just a calm surreal detachment as we did what we had to do. But it was an amazing experience, the most natural thing in the world. Her birth was going to happen anyway, despite us, and despite anything that we did. Charlotte put the child onto her breast and she started suckling immediately, a tiny bean-like bundle with eyes squeezed tightly shut. We wrapped the two of them in blankets, loaded them into the car, and Charlotte walked into the hospital carrying our baby as if it was the most normal thing in the world. The doctor checked Clea over and pronounced her a perfect little infant, and it was only after that, once everything had settled down, that I started to feel that intense joy that comes with being a father to a brand new daughter. They say there are three things every man should do before he dies, so that he might have lived a full and complete life. He should plant a tree, build a house, and have a child, but I think I would change the latter to "deliver a child" instead, because it is a once-in-a-lifetime experience.

Charlotte didn't run the next day, but she did the day after that, and she's been at it ever since. Sebastian and Clea are growing up into beautiful children. They're healthy, calm, happy and intelligent, and the only thing they don't really seem passionate about so far is sports. But I think that will come later, because they've probably done enough running for now.

Stormwatchers

I have watched as steel cold skies
Thicken the horizon with a wall of tense air
Collapsing, then exhaling a harsh wind
As the first thin hard snow is slung out
Ahead of the obliteration.

I have touched the clouds from above
Where mountains reach up into the sky.
My outstretched hand has reached out for
The approaching unbelievable power.
Naked and vulnerable human skin,
Expectant, bracing, waiting,
For the snow to annihilate this fragile world
White, with a cold, harsh fury.

I have seen the earth bleeding into thunder
As black lightning bursts into flames
Against jagged rock and where
A wild and furious anger echoes
Against the laughter of immortal pain.

And then, finally, I saw
Each storm as a composition of music:
Always different but always the same,
With prelude, development and climax:
Completed by endless cycles of cannon and fugue
Of wind and snow, and sleet and rain,
Each melody perfect, and unique,
Each one a perfect storm.

AdK

A Scream in Stone

Patagonia is the name of the final, slender 2000-kilometre stretch of South America, as it tapers into the tempestuous confluence of three oceans at Cape Horn. Slicing Patagonia in half, the southern end of the Andes mountain range runs like the spine of a dragon, dividing Chile to the west from Argentina to the east. A spectacular ridge of gnarly rock, this dragon's-back mountain range is almost continually battered by the gales and storms that blow in from the west and caps of ice mark its long spine on the Chilean side. Patagonia is a tempestuous place with the most atrocious mountain weather in the world.

Of all the spectacular rock peaks in Patagonia, the Cerro Torre is the most beautiful. It's not the highest but it is the finest and most elegant. It is a slender, needle-like spire with sweeping granite walls etched with rime ice, soaring into the sky to hold aloft what seems like an impossibly balanced mushroom of ice on the very summit. In Spanish *cerro torre* simply means "Mountain Tower", but I've always thought of it as a natural sculpture with perfect form. If a mountain peak were to have emotions, Cerro Torre would be tortured and anguished, condemned as it is to be eternally trapped in the vertical plane, shackled by ice and continually battered and torn by the fury of the elements.

This incredible tension between rock and storm must have inspired Reinhold Messner, famed for his Himalayan climbing achievements, to describe Cerro Torre as a "Scream in Stone". Like an Eduard Munch masterpiece, it is a perfect description of a perfect peak.

For years I had dreamed of standing on Cerro Torre's summit. As a climber nothing attracts me more than sharp needles of rock that are seemingly impossible to climb, and the Torre held a powerful magnetic attraction that gripped my imagination and desire.

Julie felt a similar pull and together we set out on a four-month trip to Argentina with our main ambition being to climb Cerro Torre. We made a few stops along the way, like climbing Aconcagua, the highest peak in the Andes, but on Christmas Day we walked into the Cerro Torre base camp in the forests below the mountain. The whispering wind through the Magellan beech trees belied the howling tempest of wind and snow higher up. We quietly set up our base camp below Laguna Torre and made ourselves comfortable because we knew we would be there for a while. I took a deep breath and settled into the rhythm of Patagonian days.

There is an infamous mystery surrounding Cerro Torre that is unresolved to this day. In 1959 an ambitious and flamboyant Italian by the name of Cesare Maestri claimed to have made the first ascent of the spire via a masterly rush up the vertiginous north east face. Nicknamed Ragno delle Dolomiti, the Spider of the Dolomites, and a man who once famously declared that he always made love in the press-up position to keep fit, his claim has drawn controversy ever since. At the time his Austrian partner, ice-climbing wizard Toni Egger, was killed in an ice avalanche on the descent. Maestri himself was found half-alive, face down in the snow, at the foot of the face by a third team member, Cesarino Fava, who had waited for the two to return for six days in a snow cave at the base. Maestri gave a harrowing account of their swift ascent on thick ice and their climb was lauded the world over as an unparalleled achievement in mountaineering.

Maestri returned to Italy a hero, receiving a medal for bravery, but within a few years doubts about the veracity of his claim began to creep in. Cracks and inconsistencies appeared in Maestri's account, his details of the upper part of their climb were vague and sketchy, and the facts kept changing about where the line of ascent went and how many pitons and bolts were or weren't used. There was no proof of their climb because the camera used for summit pictures had been lost, swept away with Egger in the avalanche. But Maestri kept insisting, despite mounting evidence against him, that theirs was a legitimate ascent. It remains controversial.

It was only in 2005, after many attempts by world-class alpinists, that three Italians, veteran climber Ermanno Salvaterra with Alessandro Beltrami, and Rolo Garibotti, finally summitted the route that Maestri claimed to have climbed. They found no evidence of Maestri's ascent on the upper reaches: no pitons, wedges, or anchors of any kind that they would have used for their descent. However, low down on the mountain they found Maestri's hammer together with a stash of gear. Round One in the bitter contest to climb the Torre was deemed a "disputed ascent", to Maestri's ongoing rancour.

In the decade following Maestri's climb, criticism mounted, especially from his arch rivals, the legendary Italian alpinists Walter Bonatti and Carlo Mauri, the first men to have climbed Gasherbrum 4 in the Himalayas. They had been Maestri's bitter rivals in the race to be first to climb Cerro Torre. Mauri went as far as to suggest that Maestri's ascent had been fabricated. Stung by these slurs on his honour, Maestri returned to the mountain in 1971, 12 years after his "first ascent". This time his eyes were set on the southeast flank of the peak, a beautiful, aesthetic line and the obvious route on the east side, bar long sections of completely blank rock.

On this expedition he brought with him a large crew of ten climbers and, even more controversially at the time, a cumbersome petrol-driven air compressor, which they hauled up behind them to power the drill they used to bolt their way across the blank rock. After heinous struggles with the weather and frostbite, Maestri and his team reached the top of the rock wall. However they chose not to summit the ice mushroom claiming, "It's just a lump of snow. It'll blow away one day." Maestri broke off the bolts on the final 30 metres as a challenge to future climbers and as justification for the extreme engineering he had done. The compressor they left hanging high on the wall just under the summit. Little did he know that his bolt ladder would create a furore in climbing circles, sparking an ethical debate about climbing by fair means. So much so that the British press condemned his ascent as "akin to catching a cable car up Mont Blanc and then fooling yourself into believing you have climbed it". Round Two became known as a technically incomplete ascent, much to Maestri's disgust.

Cerro Torre was definitively climbed for the first time in 1974 by another Italian, Casimiro Ferrari, via the ice-plastered West Face on the Chilean side. And Maestri's compressor route was completed to the summit, on top of the ice mushroom, in 1981 by the American big wall climber, Jim Bridwell. He deftly used pure aid techniques to bypass the final 30 metres of sabotaged bolts. So the tally in the end became two out of four to the mountain, or four out of four to the climbers, no one knows for sure.

Climbing achievements have always been based on honour: if you claim to have climbed something, most climbers will accept it at face value because there is no reason why they shouldn't. Anyone making a false claim is only deceiving themselves. So, I've often questioned Maestri's ascents. Why did he feel compelled to return to redo this beautiful peak with a drill if he had already summitted it as he claimed? And why has he been known to say that he wished he had died on Cerro Torre and that it would give him pleasure if the mountain were smashed to pieces and yet he claims his ascent was "the most important endeavour in the world"? And if he hadn't climbed it, why would he lie about that first ascent, especially since his partner had been killed? To me, there is nothing in the world, no honour, fame or glory, that can make up for the loss of a friend's life in climbing, but I guess Maestri felt differently.

An American friend of mine, Jim Donini, was ascending Torre Egger, Cerro Torre's neighbour named in Egger's memory, when he discovered parts of Toni Egger's body in the glacier 18 years after the accident. The grisly photo he showed me of Egger's leg bone sticking out of his leather boot brought home to me the tragedy and the very human cost of the controversy. Was it worth it? Was it pure ambition to be the first man up Cerro Torre that drove Maestri to the lengths to which he went? He is a man beset by demons, perhaps of his own making like Raskolnikov in Dostoyevsky's *Crime and Punishment*, and I believe it is eating him alive. He remains closed and non-committal to this day, refusing to speak about the climb, and insisting that it is a point of honour that his word be taken as the truth. In 1998 my American friend, Mark Synott, travelled to Italy on assignment for the American magazine *Climbing* to interview Maestri and find out what really happened. He came away no wiser, telling me later that Maestri was like a closed book, a man who was concealing something. Unfortunately he'll take the truth with him to the grave and Cerro Torre will always keep his secret in a wind-torn scream of stone.

Sometimes I fancied I could hear history in those winds – sounds, voices, and laughter – but it was only the wind playing tricks with my imagination. Cerro Torre stands aloof to our human dramas in a cloud capped maelstrom, the only sounds being the ripping shriek of wind on rock.

Julie and I had come to climb the southeast ridge, Maestri's compressor route because, despite all the drama and history, it is the easiest and quickest way up what would otherwise be a very difficult peak. Without Maestri and his drill, the number of successful ascents of Cerro Torre could probably be counted on one hand. We moved our climbing equipment up to a bivouac two hours below the start of the route and then settled into our base camp as a 20-day storm rumbled in. In Patagonia, days are like hours; they melt into each other and suddenly weeks have slipped by. But each day brings a climber closer to the mountain. An almost spiritual affinity unique to Patagonia develops, the peaks become ever more precious and people, drawn by the spirit of the place, return year after year.

Four Austrians shared our camp. Tommi Bonapace and Toni Panholzer had been making repeated attempts on Maestri's original 1959 route on the North Side for the past four seasons. If you tallied it all up, they had spent more than a year camped in the beech forest and had made dozens of attempts without success. Toni hailed from Linz, the same town in Austria as Toni Egger, and he believed implicitly that Maestri and Egger had succeeded on the first ascent. They were archetypal frontiersmen, long-haired, rough-looking, bearded wild men, but very good climbers. Their friends, the cleaner-cut Florian Bruckner and Rudi Cassel had come to climb the compressor route like us. The four of them lived in a dark, smoky, plastic-sheeted hut built around a clump of trees like hobbits and occasionally walked out to the nearest village to restock their food supplies.

During the many idle days of waiting for good weather, we carved wooden pipes to smoke our dry Argentinean tobacco, made bread on the fire and grew to be friends. We hiked in the forest, exercised by doing pull-ups and sit-ups and had a great time. Never once was I bored in Patagonia. Julie and I had brought an entire duffel bag filled with books. We made a sizeable dent in the pile, but never got to the bottom. Simply watching the hurtling clouds over the Torres could keep me occupied for hours on end. I think that in order to succeed in Patagonia you have to accept the terms set by the mountain. You have to settle in and learn how to be patient, because if you don't the end result will be acute boredom and probably bitter failure. Patagonian days are timeless.

A few months before we arrived in Patagonia, Cerro Torre had been the scene of a movie shoot. It's not the easiest of locations but at least they were filming *in situ*. Led by Reinhold Messner and the acclaimed filmmaker Werner Hertzog, the crew had used helicopters and fixed ropes to make a big budget mountaineering drama entitled *Schrei aus Stein* (Scream of Stone), the plot roughly following the dispute over Maestri's first ascent of the mountain. For some reason Messner wanted to take the compressor back to a museum in Europe, so they hauled it up to the mushroom ice cap to be collected by helicopter, but before they could fly in a big storm blew in and buried it in ice. In the end the film crew abandoned the compressor, their gear and their ropes on the wall.

As we waited, the storms continued to roar in from the west and the barometer rose and fell. We had several false starts and two serious attempts on Cerro Torre – each one ending in a minor epic as the weather slammed us into retreat. On the first occasion Julie's sleeping bag was ripped out of her hands by a gust of wind that sent it into a horrifying pirouette hundreds metres out into the cold sky before the approaching storm. On the second, I watched the bolts I was hanging on freeze into a thick baton of ice within minutes as the winds plastered the wall with rime ice. Our two failed attempts forced us to rethink and to opt for a streamlined plan to start at night and to climb continuously until we reached the top, and then to rappel down the following night.

On our third try the weather was perfect. We left the bivvy rocks at 3am and 600 metres of mixed climbing put us onto the southeast col, known as the Col of Patience, moments before the sun rose to a glorious day. Above the col, we climbed nine rope lengths of alternating rock and snow, and by noon we had reached the first of Maestri's bolt ladders, which made a stuttering pathway up and across the blank rock. He had drilled small round holes into which he'd hammered square iron spikes that had an eye on one end. I had seen this type of bolt before in the Dolomites in Italy and it brought home to me the hard substance of Maestri's burning desire to reach the top. It had taken enormous determination to do that much drilling and, as we clipped into the piton eyes and climbed upwards, I was thankful that they were there. We made rapid progress up the featureless rock. The sun was melting the ice above us and with a continual roar, shards of ice crashed down the East Face. We ducked them all, fearlessly climbing as fast as we could. Our two Austrian friends were a pitch ahead and all of us were incredibly psyched to be going for it with an energy that was palpable. Higher up, we wound our way through bizarre suspended gargoyles of rime ice that had been pasted onto the mountain by the wind, as late afternoon shadows were cast across the face. I felt really happy. The climbing was straightforward and our exposed position was spectacular. We climbed up to the final headwall of vertical rock, a 200-metre face marked with a machine-gunned row of bolts that would take us to the summit.

Two pitches from the top, the peaks of Fitzroy and Poincenot blazed fiery pink across the valley from us as night fell. I had just turned my headlamp on when the full moon rose from behind Piedra del Fraile. Never before had I experienced such a place. Darkness plunged away on both sides as the moon lit the night sky and suspended us in a surreal and vertical world. It was amazing. This, I thought, was the essence of the Patagonian experience. This was the reason people wait a whole year to climb a single route. Alpinism is sometimes rewarded with such precious moments as these, moments that are hardly ever repeated, but which remain as powerful images burnt indelibly into our memory.

We climbed one more bolt ladder up to the famous last pitch, now known as the Bridwell Pitch, the scene of the chopped bolts and the final belay where Maestri had left his compressor. But the compressor was missing, still buried in the ice somewhere above our heads, and a fixed rope left by the German film crew hung down the wall.

Hanging there from three bolts in the dark moonlight, we could have been on any wall in the world, except that the magnetic attraction of Cerro Torre suddenly clicked into force. I was almost manic to be so close, terrified of not summiting. Summit fever is a curious thing. My prize, my dream, was so close I would have done anything to reach the top. My ethics plunged to the glacier below and for want of saving the half hour it would take us to climb on delicate aid gear, I gave in to my ambition and jumared up the rope hanging there so seductively in the night.

We climbed up to the top of the ice mushroom and looked down at the silver, moon-illuminated plateau of the Hielo Continental and the Chilean ice cap at midnight. It was an incredible sight in the soft grey moonlight, one of those rare occasions when I wished my eyes could store the images like a camera because I'll never see them again in that way. Spires, like sharp fangs, punctured the air all around us, draped with ghostly cloaks of snow and ice. We were in an unreal world and I felt like I was sleepwalking or in some kind of dream.

We didn't linger on the summit because it was cold and an inhospitable wind had slipped in off the ice cap. We rappelled back down the headwall and chopped out a small ledge in the ice towers to rest and brew tea. We decided to wait for daylight before continuing down, because both of us were tired and the weather looked like it would hold for a few hours longer.

Exhilaration from having climbed Cerro Torre swelled inside me as we sat there through the last of the night. I had a feeling of overflowing pride and an affirmation of something that was truly mine, an experience that no one could ever take away from me. I felt a deep affinity with the steep, rough spire on which we sat. There is no way I could ever wish the mountain to be smashed to pieces as Maestri had done. From high on the Torre, we watched the thin red line of day streak across the dark hills and the glaciers slowly lose their luminescence. In that half hour before dawn the peaks seemed softer, more intimate and so very alive in their gentle awakening, but that might have been my elated imagination. At first light we rappelled down, reaching our bivvy rocks late in the afternoon. I looked back up and Cerro Torre still looked impossible to climb. I couldn't believe we had been up there just a few hours earlier.

We came down to base camp and I started to feel depressed. True, we had climbed a beautiful mountain but it had not been in a worthy style. Pulling on bits and pieces of the film crew's fixed ropes and finally jumaring the Bridwell pitch left me feeling unsettled, like I had cheated. I had overstepped the boundaries of my own ethical definition of climbing but I had come a little closer to understanding how the Torre has become such a tower of controversy. I had felt the summit lure and enough surging ambition to elbow my ethics aside, and I realised that the line between truth and falsity in Maestri's claim to have climbed the North Ridge was razor thin. It could have gone either way, but I think that his claim is false. I feel sorry for Maestri if he did indeed let ambition and desire for recognition overcome his honesty, because climbing is an ultimate form of truth. Up there in the wind everything is laid bare, including your soul.

Removing compressors by helicopter has no justification, but then again neither does climbing fixed ropes. Our four Austrian friends felt so strongly and demanded so forcefully that the mountain be restored to its original, historical condition that a helicopter was provided by the film crew to set things straight. Some weeks later the best day of the entire season dropped on us unexpectedly. It was a magic day with blue skies and no wind, a Patagonian gift. Julie and I were climbing the Torre Innominata across the glacier when we saw the Austrians being dropped off on the summit of Cerro Torre by helicopter: four tiny dots impossibly stranded on top of the ice-mushroom, incomparably diminished by the sweeping big walls. They dug out the compressor and, using their ropes, they lowered it back down to its original spot at the last belay. Then they rappelled down the route, removing all the shredded bits of old fixed rope.

They sacrificed a perfect climbing day because they believed in their ethics and because they wanted the Torre to be left as it should be, a beautiful citadel full of history and meaning. I am pleased that there are people like that, people to whom the mountains are greater than the sum of their ambitions. With its raw and savage beauty, Cerro Torre embodies a call to all climbers to be true to themselves and to climb mountains in good style for the right reasons. We have to listen to that call because after we have all gone Cerro Torre will still be there, a precious spire poised right on the brink of storm like a scream in stone.

Glossary

Aguille Pinnacle in French. Usually very nice, exposed summits.

Aid Hanging onto equipment for means of ascent when it's too difficult to free climb. Sometimes it's the only way up something.

Alpinisim A mountain-climbing style developed in the Alps, it involves climbing to the top in one push, carrying everything with you. It's the purest form of climbing a peak.

Arête A sharp edge or outside corner, like the outside corner of a building, an airy and aesthetic place to climb.

BASE jump An acronym for Building, Antenna, Span and Earth, it's a jump from any fixed object, typically a cliff, building, antenna tower or bridge, using a parachute to save you from a sticky end.

Belay To hold the end of a climber's rope in case they fall. Various types of mechanical braking devices are used for belaying.

Bivouac An overnight stop, often in inhospitable places.

Bolt Ordinarily used in construction, it's a fixed device that is inserted into drilled holes and then tightened, creating a solid point of protection. Bolts are great to clip into because you know they are bombproof.

Cam A mechanical device with spring-loaded cams used for protection. This device is squeezed and inserted into a crack, whereupon the cams spring open, gripping the sides of the rock and holding it in place. A very versatile form of protection and easy to place.

Canopy A BASE parachute is highly specialised and made specifically for the stress loading of jumping from fixed objects.

Carabiner A metal snap link. You never have enough on aid climbs.

Corner A feature of rock folded inwards, usually climbable. (See Dihedral)

Crampons Spikes attached to the boots used for ice climbing. Tread carefully.

Crux The hardest section of a climb.

Dihedral The inside corner where two planes of rock meet at 90 degrees. Nice to climb because you can usually span your legs across both sides and take some weight off your arms.

Epic An exceedingly disagreeable experience.

Flare Method of stopping forward movement while BASE jumping, either in freefall or under canopy.

Hardware Metal climbing gear, pitons, cams, carabiners, etcetera, which can get quite heavy if you take a lot, but it can also be scary if you take too little.

Haulbag A sturdy sack for equipment, which is pulled up behind you on a rope. Often nicknamed "The Pig" or "The Bastard" because they can be a pain to haul when they get stuck.

Ice screw A form of protection screwed into ice, which is strenuous to place when you are hanging off your ice axe on vertical ice.

Jumar Colloquial name used for a Swiss brand of sliding ascender clamp. Jumars don't stick to iced-up ropes, but other types of ascenders do.

Lead (a pitch) The first person climbing leads the rope out as they go, inserting protection into the rock or ice to safeguard themselves. It's the most challenging part of climbing, because should they fall, they will drop double the distance they have lead out from the last protection point.

Peg/Piton A metal spike hammered into a crack in the rock for protection. Sometimes difficult to remove, that's why you see so many of them fixed.

Pilot chute A small drogue that inflates with air and deploys the main parachute.

Pitch A section of climbing, either as long as the rope (usually 60 metres), or between convenient features or belay anchors.

Portaledge Portable stretchers made from an aluminium frame and a nylon mat. They are suspended from a single point and are used for sleeping on.

Pumped Tired forearms, the severity of which depends on how fit you are.

Rack A selection of equipment of various sizes to be slotted, fitted or hammered into the rock and used for protection against falling off the mountain. Be careful not to drop it, because then you can't get up or down.

Rail Horizontal crack. If you can climb inside it, it's called a dassie traverse.

Rappel A French word for descent by sliding down the rope. The German word is abseil. Remember to tie a knot at the end of the rope. Rapelling is scary and dangerous.

Rivets Metal sleeves that are hammered into drilled holes and used for aid.

Sky hook A curved piece of metal hooked onto the rock and then hung on for aid climbing, which is downright terrifying.

Sliding ascender clamp A device that is used to climb up ropes. It can be slid upwards but locks tight when weight is applied. It is very strenuous. (See Jumar)

Sport climbing Climbing using bolts for protection. Because they always hold falls, grades of climbing difficulty can be pushed a lot higher.

Track Body position in freefall, hands at your sides and legs outstretched, making you move forward.

Verglas A thin film of slick, transparent ice that is desperately slippery.

Wall climbing Climbing a long rock face, usually involving nights spent on the cliff and a lot of hard work.

Wingsuit Flying suit that fills with air turning the body into a wing. Very difficult to learn to fly it, because you have to fly it to learn.

Photographic credits

The copyright © of the photographs rests with the following photographers and/or their agents.

Numbering pertains to the order of appearance of the photographs within the pictorial sections.

Sandy Britain: 45; **Julie Brugger:** page 5 (left), 1, 2, 35, 36, 37, 38, 39, 40, 41, 42, 57, 77, 78, 79; **Jimmy Chin (www.jimmychin.com):** 4, 8, 65; **Juliette de Combs:** 28, 30; **Andy de Klerk:** 27, 29, 31, 32, 33, 66, 67, 68, 69, 70, 71, 72, 73, 74; **Cameron Ewart-Smith/***Getaway***:** back cover, page 5 (right), 50, 51, 52, 53, 54, 55, 56, 76; **Ed February Collection:** 5, 6, 7, 22, 24, 26, 43, 48, 58, 59, 60, 61, 62; **Nic Good:** 12, 13; **Karl Hayden Collection:** 9, 10, 14, 34; **Xandi Kreuzeder (www.xandikreuzeder.de):** page 2; **Tony Lourens:** 46, 47; **Charley Mace:** 75; **Bobby Model/M-11 (www.bobbymodel.com):** front cover, spine, pages 6–7, 15, 16, 17, 18, 19, 20, 21, 23, 25, 44; **Peter Samuelson:** 49, 63, 64, 82; **Mark Seuring:** 80, 81; **Dion Tromp:** 3, 11.

Illustrations by Peter Samuelson. Topo diagrams by Andy de Klerk, graphics enhancement by Peter Samuelson.